praying for keeps

Praying for Keeps

Published by Serendipity House Publishers
Nashville, Tennessee

In cooperation with Fellowship Church Resources
Dallas, Texas

ISBN: 1-5749-4146-1

Dewey Decimal Classification: 248.32
Subject Headings:
PRAYER \ BIBLE-STUDY \ CHRISTIAN LIFE

SERENDIPITY® HOUSE

1-800-525-9563
www.SerendipityHouse.com

Fellowship Church .com

www.fellowshipchurch.com

Printed in the United States of America
10 09 08 07 06 05 04 1 2 3 4 5 6 7 8 9 10

contents

how to use this book

Small groups are a vital part of how we do ministry at Fellowship Church just as they are in many churches around the world. There are a number of different theories on how small groups should work, and they are all great in different ways. The book you are holding is written with our model in mind. So take a minute to read the following explanation, then feel free to adapt as necessary.

Each of our small groups practices a three-part agenda in every meeting. That agenda includes a social time, a discussion time, and a prayer time. Each of these elements share equal importance, but not necessarily equal time. To help you get the most out of this book, we have included an explanation of each of the parts.

The first element of every small-group meeting should be a time of socializing. This phase of the meeting should be about 30% of your time together. Welcome everyone as they arrive at the host home; make visitors feel welcome by introducing yourself and showing genuine interest in them. Enjoy some snacks, or if your group prefers, a meal together. Then move on to the second part of the meeting—the lesson.

The lesson itself may take as much as 50% of your group's meeting time. You may want to start this phase with a short "icebreaker" to get everyone talking. The questions in the "Start It Up" section of each session are what we refer to as "level the playing field" questions that everyone can participate in, regardless of their level of spiritual maturity or Bible knowledge. As your group moves through the "Talk It Up" section in each meeting, remember that it is more important to finish on time than to finish each question. It is okay to skip some questions to allow enough time to take care of the third phase of the small-group time: "Lift It Up."

The "Lift It Up" section is a vital part of every small-group meeting and should take about 20% of your time. You will be able to share with the group what God is doing in your life as well as asking the group to support you in specific prayers. To help focus this time, there are one or two questions that will prompt prayers based on the material you just covered. There is also a space for you to write down your prayer requests so you don't forget them and so you can communicate them clearly when it is your turn. Below that is a place to write down the prayer requests of the people in your group so you can remember to pray for each request throughout the week.

As an additional tool to assist you in your spiritual development journey, 10 devotionals lead up to each of the Sessions 2 through 6. Ten devotionals are provided to accommodate groups that meet every other week, giving material for five days each week during that two-week interval. These will help you develop a daily quiet time with God. To get the absolute most from this book, I challenge you to take 5 or 10 minutes a day to read and apply these devotionals in your life.

God's best!
Ed

praying for keeps

When our oldest daughter Lee Beth was three years old, she wanted a baby brother or sister so badly that it was all she thought about. She had an unrealistic picture, though, of what it would be like to help change diapers, bottle feed, and rock a baby to sleep. And in Lee Beth's mind, only two things kept her from having that brother or sister—Mommy and Daddy.

One Sunday morning before church, she asked her mother if she was ever going to be a big sister. Lisa explained to her that if it was in God's plan for our family to grow, then it would happen. But in the meantime, she explained, Lee Beth should pray to God and talk to Him about it.

So Lee Beth, taking my wife's cue, immediately walked down the hallway to her room, went to her play kitchenette, and picked up the little plastic phone. Lisa peered around the corner just in time to hear the one-way conversation that went something like this: "God, hi. This is Lee Beth. I just want you to know that I really want a baby brother or sister. And if you would give me one, that would be great. And if not, I'll be happy with my dolls. Well, I'll talk to you again a little later. Bye."

Lee Beth didn't worry that she hadn't said the most eloquent words; she didn't concern herself with a fear that God might not hear her prayer. And, most importantly, she surrendered the situation to God's will, not her own. We adults could learn a lot from this simple, faith-filled example.

Prayer should be that open, honest, and available for all of us. We shouldn't have any fear, timidity, or uneasiness in going before God in prayer. The problem, though, is that many of us have misconceptions about prayer that hinder us from experiencing the personal connection with God that we long for. We look at prayer through a warped lens.

Over the next several weeks, we are going to debunk some of the myths and misunderstandings about prayer. We're going to learn that prayer is the believer's lifeline to a personal connection with Christ. And we'll find out that prayer can and will change the trajectory of our lives—when we pray for keeps.

session one

SMALL-GROUP SESSION

Prayer Conditioning: Shaping Up Your Prayer Life

Matthew 6:5-13; Psalm 103:13

There are a variety of different viewpoints on prayer. The sheer number of viewpoints points out that many people, even Christians, don't understand what this prayer thing is all about. For example, some of us view God as Aladdin's genie. We pray, we rub the lamp, and he zips out saying, "Your wish is my command." Others view prayer more like a fast food restaurant. Life is just busy and full of pressure. We are in a hurry, so we dash up to the drive-through window and hear a voice that sounds like it's God's say, "Welcome to prayer, may I help you?" We respond with, "Sure, God, I'd like a McBlessing with an ice-cold cola." God asks, "Would you like that with a full meal?" and we say, "No thanks, I've gotta run." Still others see prayer like a 911 call, to be used only in the event of an emergency. Unless there is a disaster, we feel fully sufficient to handle our lives. Some even think that prayer is a means of convincing God to do what we want, so we rapidly fire off arguments and case law exhibits like an attorney in a courtroom.

All of these images are misconceptions. God has something very different in mind when He talks about prayer. It is far more than just getting what you want. It is way beyond being an emergency lifeline. Prayer is about a relationship and communication.

Start It Up

Adam and Eve walked and talked with God in the garden of Eden every evening, but since sin entered the world, our relationship with God has been broken. In order to communicate with Him, we need to reestablish that relationship and learn how to pray.

1. **Were you taught to pray as a child? Did you learn set prayers to recite, or did you learn to pray spontaneously?**

2. **How would you rate your "prayer proficiency" now? Do you think that your early training was a help or a hindrance?**

Talk It Up

Many of us today are living from day to day wondering why our lives aren't really coming together. We don't feel the peace that passes all understanding. We don't feel like we have a purpose or real strength in the situations we face, and we don't know which way to turn. The answer to all of these problems is prayer. We will never be the kind of people that we were meant to be unless we learn how to communicate with God.

Most of us are aware that if we truly want to know something, we should ask an expert. Jesus' disciples obviously realized this, and one day, after observing Jesus praying, they asked, "Lord, teach us to pray ..." (Luke 11:1).

If you want to experience the awesome power of prayer, there are four basic "prayer conditions" that you and every other believer in Jesus Christ have to meet. You must understand the purpose of prayer, make prayer a top priority, pray with the right motives, and take advantage of a plan.

Condition 1: Understand the Purpose of Prayer

Prayer is not about asking God to do our will. Instead, it helps to bring us into conformity with God's will. Prayer is one important vehicle through which God has chosen to share with us His purpose and direction for the world. God wants us to pray, and He is waiting for us to talk with Him often.

Read Matthew 6:9-13

When we see and hear the words "our Father," they may not mean much to many of us. We have heard again and again that God is our father. However, when Jesus uttered those two words, it exploded the religious tradition of His day. Jesus actually gave us permission to call the almighty God of the universe "Father," just as a child calls for his "Daddy." Do you know God in an intimate way? Do you know Him well enough to call Him your daddy or father? If you are a parent, you know there is nothing you like to hear better than your child calling your name in love and trust. Do you realize that the Almighty God is inviting you into that kind of relationship? There is no voice that He likes to hear more than the voice of his child calling, "Father!"

Read Psalm 103:13

Many times this concept of the fatherhood of God is difficult for people to grasp because they grew up with a father who did not fulfill his role. Some have had an abusive father, or one who was terribly inconsistent or domineering, or perhaps one who ignored his children altogether. We can subconsciously lay our earthly father's character qualities onto our Heavenly Father's shoulders, and then say, "If God is like my earthly father, I don't want any part of Him. Fathers are no good." We need to turn our thinking around. God is not like just any father. He is the measure by which we know what a true father is. Good fathers are a reflection of God, and bad fathers are bad because they fall far short of God's model. God is a compassionate father. He loves His children. Romans 8:17 tells us that "If we are [God's] children, then we are heirs—heirs of God and co-heirs with Christ." That means we have access to everything that God has. If we know the Son, and through Him, the Father, then we can call God our father too. We can communicate with Him, and we can tap into all His resources. God shares His riches with His children.

3. What are some characteristics of good earthly fathers that you have known? In what ways do these men reflect God, the Father?

4. Do you see the Lord's Prayer in Matthew 6 as something that we should recite verbatim, or as a model prayer from which we should build our prayers? Why?

Condition 2: Make Prayer a Top Priority

Prayer was a priority in the life of Jesus; it should be a priority in our lives as well. Any time we read the Bible, we should be looking to see what things are a big deal to God. People matter to God, so people should matter to us. Truth matters to God, so we should seek the truth and reject lies. Communicating in prayer matters to God, so prayer should matter to us.

Can you imagine what would happen if you decided to skip communicating with your boss for the next month? Or how about your coach, or teacher? No e-mail. No faxes. No phone conversations. No contact whatsoever. It wouldn't be a great success, would it? We couldn't effectively do our jobs. We wouldn't be in touch with what was happening in other parts of the business. We would lose the motivation to get our work done. Prayer is not just a command, a "good work," or a rule to follow. It is our lifeline! If you are struggling with lack of direction in your life, or if you feel like you are floundering and don't know which way to turn next, maybe it's because you are failing to communicate with your "Boss." Maybe you are neglecting the advice of your "Coach," or ignoring your "Teacher." We need to ask ourselves this question: when we get to heaven, and stand before God, are we going to see a huge pile of blessings, with a tag on them that reads, "Never Asked For"? Are we going to find that we missed out on the best part of life because we never bothered to make connecting with God a priority in our lives?

5. What do you think a life with real "prayer priority" would look like?

Condition 3: Pray with the Right Motives

Read Matthew 6:5-8

When we actually do make prayer a priority—when we set out to communicate with God regularly and often—it feels good. It is encouraging to know that we are doing something right, the way God intended it. Unfortunately, as humans, we will be tempted to advertise this great change in our lives. We will want to start dropping little comments to let other people know that we have regular appointments with the King of the universe. "I get up an hour earlier now, so I can pray longer before I leave for work." "I just couldn't get along without my half hour prayer time before breakfast."

Jesus gave His disciples a special warning about this temptation. Prayer is not something meant to be paraded out in front of everyone. We are not supposed to stand on the street corners, proudly proclaiming to everyone just how holy we are. Instead, Jesus instructed us to find a "closet," a private quiet place, and do our praying there. Remember, prayer is about a relationship. It isn't about gaining points in heaven for the number of hours we put in. It isn't about gaining a reputation on earth as a "great prayer warrior," or letting other people know how faithful we are. If we are praying with these kinds of attitudes, then we are praying with selfish motives. Such prayers are going to go about as far as the ends of our noses, and then fall flat. Why should God reward us when we have already rewarded ourselves?

6. What might be some other advantages of a personal "prayer closet"? What places have you found that make good "closets"?

Condition 4: Take Advantage of a Plan

When God inspired Paul to teach the Corinthian church about orderly worship, He said, "everything should be done in a fitting and orderly way" (1 Corinthians 14:40). While the context of this verse specifically applies to public worship, we can also apply it to our personal prayer lives. Because God is our Father, we are free to come and talk to Him at any time, even when we don't know what to say. In fact, He has assured us that when we don't know what to pray for, the Holy Spirit will intercede for us, and translate our troubled feelings "with groans that words cannot express" (Romans 8:26). At the same time, it can be helpful to us to plan our prayers. As humans, many of us struggle with a short attention span, a mind which wanders, and uncertainty about how we should pray. A plan can help to keep our prayer times on track, but sometimes we plan our prayers so we can articulate eloquent, persuasive prayers that will impress God and the people around us. We somehow think that He is more likely to answer if our prayers are well-worded. That's not the point of a plan.

7. How can we avoid "babbling" when we pray? What might this look like?

8. Since God knows what we need before we ask for it, why do we need to ask? How does knowing this affect how we pray?

Invite to be involved

P-R-A-Y

Especially as we are learning how to pray, it can be helpful to order our prayers around this acronym:

Praise
Repent
Ask
Yield

ACTS
adoration
confession
thanksgiving
supplication

The first thing we should do when we talk with God is to praise Him. Praise is expressing our love and adoration to God. In praise, we concentrate on His character and attributes. Part of praise is also thanking Him. Don't just say, "Thank-you-for-all-the-blessings-Amen." Be specific. Let God know exactly what you are thankful for and why. This will set the right tone and context for the rest of your prayer time.

The "R" of PRAY stands for repent. Confession is the first step in repentance. We must learn the art of confession. Most of us want to generalize and take shortcuts when we pray. We want to toss all of our sins into a giant heap, and say, "Lord, there is the garbage dump. Forgive all my sins and sweep this trash out of my life." That seems like the easy way. After all, God already knows what all the sins are. He can forgive the whole pile at once, and we won't have to look at the mess again. But actually, looking at the garbage is the point of confession and repentance. God wants us to look at our sins, to see them as sins, and to individually, one by one, confess those sins to Him and then repent or turn away from them. Until we actually take a close-up look at who we really are and what we really do, we won't be willing to change. We will revisit the same sins—the same garbage dump—over and over again. Repentance means turning from sin; it means changing direction and leaving the garbage behind.

"A" stands for ask. Ask God for the things you need. We sometimes think that since God already knows what we need, there is no need to ask. But God wants us to ask Him. He said, "Ask, and it will be given to you, seek and you will find" (Luke 11:9), and "If any of you lacks wisdom, he should ask God, who gives generously to all without finding fault, and it will be given to him" (James 1:5). Being a believer is about a relationship. We are not issued a perpetual meal ticket, a full set of blessings, and a suit of spiritual armor, so that we can charge off to do our own thing. We are designed to be in constant communication with our Lord, and we are supposed to ask Him for the things we need as we need them.

"Y" stands for yield. We must yield ourselves daily to the Lord in every area of our lives. That means saying, "I want your will not mine. I will do whatever you want me to do in this situation. I am yours." We will have to keep saying this over and over again. Yielding isn't a once and for all action. Every morning, every afternoon, every time a difficult situation comes up, we will have to say again just as Jesus did, "Not as I will, but as you will [Father]" (Matthew 26:39). Ask your Father to help you be like Jesus.

Lift It Up

As you are learning to make prayer a regular part of your life, one of the best things that you can do is keep a prayer journal. Write out the things you pray for, and then, when you receive answers, record those too. In a month or two, look back over the things you have prayed about. You will be amazed and encouraged to see how God has been working in your life!

9. **Regular prayer is not easy even for many Christians. What barriers keep you from praying the way you need to for yourself and for others?**

10. **Praying together for each other's needs is an important part of doing life together. In what way can this group pray for you right now and throughout the week?**

Make it a priority to pray together. Try using the P-R-A-Y method this time.

My Prayer Needs:

My Group's Prayer Needs:

June - pain + Owen's family
Nan - cousin mag. Joan
Cherie - Barbara Kinner - Ca TX -
Bruce - Melissa + family - Jerry Ransome smoke Hope - Katrina weather
Jim - Stan Gumbras - "shutting down"
Joan - Larry Fetz - Ca Prostate

before session two

DEVOTIONALS

Day 1: Matthew 6:9

This, then, is how you should pray: "Our Father in heaven, hallowed be your name."

In order to pray, we have to remember who we are talking to. God, who told us to call Him "Father," is the Creator of the universe. This familiar address shows our relationship as beloved children, who are heirs of His riches. Right after that, Jesus told us to remember who God is. "Hallowed be your name." That means that we must recognize that He is holy, and honor Him as such. God is different from His creation. He is of a different essence and a different character. He is pure and without fault, and His ways are not the same as ours. He is not only a God who loves us and wants to give to us, He is also a God who is powerful and able to answer our prayers.

Write down some of the characteristics of God that come to your mind. Take time to simply praise Him for who He is.

Day 2: Matthew 6:10

"Your kingdom come, your will be done on earth as it is in heaven."

Pray for Christ's return, and the establishment of God's ways on earth. 1 Timothy 2:2 tells us to pray for the government, so that we can live in peace, with freedom to worship Him. God wants us to be aware of His power and control even over godless governments, and to always be looking for the return of Christ.

Part of God's will being done on earth has to do with us. We are responsible to yield ourselves to Him, and do what He asks us to. We are not usually very good at this, which is why we need to ask for God's help. Sometimes, we have to pray that He will make us willing to be used, as well as asking Him for guidance.

Read 1 Thessalonians 5:4-11. Are you alert, looking forward to Christ's return? How will that affect the way you live your life today?

Day 3: Matthew 6:11

"Give us today our daily bread."

Daily bread—in this prosperous land, most of us don't have to think much about daily bread. Even when we feel that money is tight, we aren't afraid of starving. This is one of those areas where we seem to feel confident that we can provide for ourselves. We forget that all we have comes from God, and that without Him, we can do nothing. Even when we have forgotten Him, God in His goodness sends the rain, makes the crops grow, and gives us the health and strength to work for a living. God wants us to remember that we are dependent upon Him. Ask Him to keep providing you with your daily food, and remember to thank Him for His faithfulness in the past. In Romans chapter one, Paul says that God's wrath has been aroused against people who "neither glorified him as God, nor gave thanks to him." Later, Paul also admonishes us to "be thankful" (Colossians 3:15). God is a good God, providing for our daily needs even when we take it for granted. Don't forget to thank Him, acknowledging that you are helpless without Him.

Write down a list of the things that you can thank God for right now.

Day 4: Matthew 6:12

"Forgive us our debts, as we also have forgiven our debtors."

Jesus told a dramatic story to illustrate the importance of forgiveness. A man owed a huge debt to a king. It was far more than he could ever hope to repay, and he was brought trembling before his creditor. He knew that he, his wife, and his children would be sold into slavery and all their property auctioned off in order to pay for the debt. It seemed that it was the end of everything, but the servant fell to his knees and begged for mercy. The king saw his great distress and pitied him. He not only let the man go, he canceled the debt and made him completely free.

As the man walked out of the courtroom, a free man, having just experienced incredible undeserved mercy, he saw another servant who owed him a very small debt—just a few dollars. He walked up to his fellow servant, and grabbed him by the neck. He began to choke him, saying, "Pay up!" He was unmoved by the servant's pleading, and had him thrown into prison until the debt should be paid.

When the king found out about this, he confronted the man saying, "You wicked servant, I canceled all your debt because you begged me to. Shouldn't you have had mercy on your fellow servant just as I had on you?" In his anger, he turned the man over to the jailers to be tortured, until he should pay back all he owed.

Then Jesus said, "This is how my heavenly Father will treat each of you unless you forgive your brother from your heart" (see Matthew 18:23-35).

Examine yourself. Do you think that you are harboring any unforgiveness? Don't waste any time in dealing with it.

Day 5: Matthew 6:13

"And lead us not into temptation, but deliver us from the evil one."

James 1:13-14 assures us that God will never tempt us to sin. He will, however, not always protect us from temptation. Sometimes He allows Satan—the evil one—to test us, but we are never left on our own. In the same way that we pray for our food and basic needs, we need to pray for protection from Satan, and from temptation. We need to remember our dependence on God. Without His help, we won't be strong enough to withstand temptation, or wise enough to flee from it.

What temptations are you facing right now? If there is a time or place where you feel particularly tempted, take the precaution of praying about this beforehand. Preparing yourself before you are in the situation is one of the best defenses against temptation.

Eat or not eat

Day 6: Psalm 69:1-3

Save me, O God, for the waters have come up to my neck. I sink in the miry depths, where there is no foothold. I have come to the deep waters; the floods engulf me. I am worn out calling for help; my throat is parched. My eyes fail, looking for my God.

It seems easy to pray when we have nothing but thanksgivings, and a few small requests. It is easy to glorify God when all is well. But what do we do about those times when our prayers seem to go nowhere, when God is doing things that we can't understand? What about the times we are suffering unbearable pain, when we are being dragged through terrible trials, and nothing is all right? How can we praise and thank God when all we can feel is pain and anguish? Can we talk about these things with God? The answer is a resounding "Yes!"

God does not require that our prayers be organized and sanitized. We can tell Him straight out what we are struggling with, and He will listen. Listen to the words of the Psalmist. He didn't paste on a smile and say, "I'm just a little down today, but everything is really fine." He went ahead and told the truth essentially saying, "I'm up to my neck, I think I'm going to drown in a minute, and I can't even see God!" When we are in up to our necks, God wants us to yell for help. Don't be afraid to tell Him the truth about how you feel. He knows it anyway.

How can you be fully transparent with God, yet without sinning in words or thoughts?

Day 7: Job 13:15-16

Though he slay me, yet will I hope in him; I will surely defend my ways to his face. Indeed, this will turn out for my deliverance, for no godless man would dare come before him!

Job was a man who had much to bear. He was rich, powerful, and prosperous. He had sons and daughters, donkeys and oxen, sheep, camels and servants. He feared God and served Him. It would seem that all should have been exceedingly well with him, and for a long time it was.

Then God gave Satan permission to test Job, and see whether his faith was real, or only the product of prosperity. In a very few days, all of Job's possessions and children were gone, and to crown it all, he himself was afflicted with painful sores all over his body. Job was miserable, but he did not take the advice of his foolish wife: to curse God and die. His faith was real, so he knew that God must have a reason for what was happening to him. Job did not mind expressing his anguish, however, so he went on for chapters and chapters describing his misery. To help matters along, Job's three friends came to commiserate with him, and spent chapters and chapters telling him that if he would only repent of his sins, God would stop punishing him. Job knew that he was not harboring secret sin, and did not believe that his afflictions were a punishment from God. He knew enough about God's character, to trust in His justice despite his circumstances.

Do you know God's character well enough to trust Him in the face of unexplainable pain? If He is not trustworthy, what is left for you?

Day 8: Psalm 63:3-5

Because your love is better than life, my lips will glorify you. I will praise you as long as I live, and in your name I will lift up my hands. My soul will be satisfied as with the richest of foods; with singing lips my mouth will praise you.

While Job found hope in remembering God's justice, David, in this Psalm, rejoiced in God's love. Whenever we are wrestling with a problem that is too big to bear, and wondering why God does not take it away, the best thing that we can do is spend time thinking about God's character. He is unchanging: if He was once loving and just, He will always be loving and just. When you come to God with your messy, emotional, turbulent prayers, telling Him what is really on your heart, the next step is to look back at who He has been and what He has done in the past.

List some ways God has been faithful to you and others in the past. How does remembering the past help you face the future?

Day 9: Romans 8:26-27

In the same way, the Spirit helps us in our weakness. We do not know what we ought to pray for, but the Spirit himself intercedes for us with groans that words cannot express. And he who searches our hearts knows the mind of the Spirit, because the Spirit intercedes for the saints in accordance with God's will.

Not only do we sometimes have messy prayers to bring before God. We will all experience times when we don't have any idea what we should pray. We only know that our hearts are in turmoil, and we need help. When that happens, all we can do is say, "Help!" The Holy Spirit will actually take our troubled feelings and "pray for us," saying for us all the things that we need to say, yet don't know how to. God knows our hearts better than we do ourselves, and He loves us perfectly. That is how He can translate our groaning, or our turbulent and anguished prayer, into what we really need.

Why is it still important to pray even when we don't know what to say?

Day 10: Psalm 40:1-3

I waited patiently for the LORD; he turned to me and heard my cry. He lifted me out of the slimy pit, out of the mud and mire; he set my feet on a rock and gave me a firm place to stand. He put a new song in my mouth, a hymn of praise to our God. Many will see and fear and put their trust in the LORD.

Time is the biggest conflict we humans have with God's ways. We are stuck in time, but God is not. We grow impatient, and don't want to have to wait for things to happen in His time. If we wait patiently, however, we will always find God faithful. He has not forgotten us. He listens to every prayer and fear, and He will come to rescue us. It isn't always as soon as we would like, and sometimes the way He rescues isn't what we expect, but we can be sure that His way is good. Don't be afraid to talk to Him, and don't be afraid to trust Him.

Prayer is such an important part of spiritual growth that we can't afford to neglect it. Commit to spending at least a few minutes of each day in prayer. Make a mark on your calendar so that you can keep track of how you are learning to be faithful in prayer.

session two

SMALL-GROUP SESSION

Vertical Reality: Being Transparent with God

2 Corinthians 13:5; Jeremiah 1:4-9; 20:7-18; Psalm 13:1-6; 46:10

Think about a typical day in your life, a typical conversation with a friend or acquaintance. "Hi, how are you?" it usually starts. "Great," you say, or "Fine." It doesn't really matter which, because you don't necessarily mean a word of it, and neither does your friend. It's what we call "casual conversation." Most of our conversations stay at this surface level; only rarely do we break through and talk about the deeper issues of life.

Start It Up

We tend to stick to surface-level conversations because it is much safer there. It doesn't take as much energy or investment in the lives of other people. We also don't have to be vulnerable, opening ourselves up to the possibility of being hurt by the way others respond ... or don't.

1. **Describe a friendship you have in which you feel comfortable going beyond surface level. How many people are in this close circle of friends?**

2. For you, what is the dividing line between "surface-level" and "deep" conversation? How often do you dive in?

Talk It Up

Unfortunately, our conversations with God tend to go pretty much along the same lines as our conversations with people. We rarely go below the surface. We stay right on the edge of the deeper waters, where our feet can touch the bottom. We gear up with our water wings, life jackets, face masks, and nose plugs, holding on for dear life to the nearest branch of seaweed. Through all our gyrations, God is inviting us to relax, to come out into deeper water, and to learn to really trust Him.

Today's discussion is going to center around something that we could call "vertical reality," that is, learning to be transparent before God. We want to learn to pray at a deep level, and to have true community and fellowship with God. The Bible reminds us over and over again, from Genesis to Revelation, that we matter to God. We matter to Him so much that He gave His only Son for us, to pay for our transgressions and bring us into a close relationship with Himself. He wants us to talk with Him, and He wants the conversation to go both ways. Learning to listen is at least as important as learning to share your life with your Father.

Look in the Mirror

To begin with, if you want to have an in-depth relationship with God, you have to know your own depths. This means that you must learn to reflect. If you want to truly seek the heart of God—to learn how to pray—you have to learn to look honestly at yourself. We all know what happens after a big football game. Everyone gets involved in extensive post-game analysis. The coaches, the players, the commentators, even the spectators rehearse and analyze what happened. They reflect on what was good, what was bad, and what could have been better.

Read 2 Corinthians 13:5

Do you ever do a "post-game analysis" on your own life? Test your faith. Before you begin to pray, pause and reflect. Go through the day's events summarizing the decisions you made, the people you met, the good things you did, the bad things you did, the things you left undone, and the blessings God sent your way. An unexamined life is likely to spiral in circles. If you don't take time to reflect, you will repeat the same mistakes over and over again.

3. **Do you consider yourself an introspective person? What are the dangers of not examining yourself? What are the dangers of too much self-examination?**

4. **How can healthy self-examination make your prayers different?**

Once we understand the importance of reflection, and commit to taking time to examine our own lives and hearts, we have taken a big step towards transparent communication with God. The next step is to learn to pour out our hearts before the Lord.

Pour Out Your Pain and Struggles

Read Jeremiah 1:4-9

Even before birth, God's hand was on Jeremiah. He was chosen as a prophet of the Lord. God promised to give him the words to say, and to protect him. For over 40 years, Jeremiah proclaimed the word of the Lord, and prophesied doom and disaster upon an unrepentant nation. Finally, the nation's priests had had enough. The chief officer of the Temple had Jeremiah beaten and put into the stocks. Jeremiah was devastated by a sense that God had betrayed him. What could Jeremiah do with these feelings of betrayal?

Read Jeremiah 20:7-18

What will you do when that routine physical turns into your worst nightmare? What are you going to do when the girl you have been dating for a year and half writes you a "Dear John" letter? What are you going to do, parents, when you have been praying for protection and suddenly your child is injured in a freak accident? What are you going to do when the foundations of your faith weaken and you feel the roof caving in?

The human response is to spin on our heels, saying, "I have had enough. In fact, I don't believe in You anymore, God. I will never darken the doors of a church again. Others who feel that they have been "burned" by God, relate to God for the rest of their lives in a guarded fashion. "God deceived me once, I will never get into that position again." Still others react with a false bravado, a fake "hallelujah anyhow" attitude. Not many of us react as Jeremiah did. He prayed a transparent prayer; not a formula prayer, not an edited and sanitized prayer, but an authentic prayer pouring out the pain and hurt from his heart.

5. **Does praying a transparent prayer feel safe to you? Why or why not?**

Jeremiah was so sure of God's character and so confident of God's love that he risked praying a transparent prayer, a prayer that was real, messy, and pain-filled. Many of us are afraid to open up like this. We fear that if we do not pray a theologically and spiritually correct prayer, God might say, "Get out of My presence." The truth is that God wants us to do as Jeremiah did. There are many other examples of transparent prayers throughout the Bible.

6. **How can we be transparent and still keep from charging God with wrongdoing?**

To help us with this, let's look at three helpful principles for transparent prayer.

(1) Read Psalm 13:1-4

Here, David shows us the first principle of transparent prayer: Recount your pain. Acknowledging and revealing your feelings to God is the first step toward healing. It is tempting for us to cover up, to pretend that we don't have the feelings of desolation, rebellion, lack of trust, or depression. We want to pray "good" prayers rather than authentic ones. Concealing our feelings from God is pretty pointless. He already knows what is really in our hearts, and He wants us to be honest enough to acknowledge the truth with Him.

(2) Read Psalm 13:5

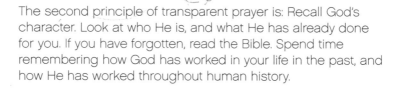

The second principle of transparent prayer is: Recall God's character. Look at who He is, and what He has already done for you. If you have forgotten, read the Bible. Spend time remembering how God has worked in your life in the past, and how He has worked throughout human history.

(3) Read Psalm 13:6

Our third and final principle is: Resolve to trust in God. David poured out his heart to God, recounting his pain. Then, he recalled what he already knew of God's person and character. Despite his deep pain and struggles, David could then end his prayer saying, "He has been good to me" because of his faith in God. We won't always understand His ways—in fact, we seldom understand fully. But we can trust His promises.

7. **What other scriptural promises, or examples of God's work in your past, can you think of that would give you confidence in praying transparently?**

8. Should anyone other than God hear your transparent prayers? Why or why not?

Soak Up God's Wisdom

Once we have learned to reflect and to pour out our hearts, God wants us to learn to listen. Prayer is meant to be a two-way conversation. God wants us to talk to Him so He can hear in our own words what we have been thinking and feeling. But He also wants to talk back to us. He wants us to listen for His instructions, His encouragement, and His redirection.

Does God still speak to people? Yes! Most of us won't hear an audible voice from God, but He can and does communicate with your spirit. He speaks to us through His Word, the Bible. God also speaks to us through relationships and through the illumination of His Holy Spirit. Sometimes it may seem hard to distinguish between God speaking to us, and our own desires or imaginations grasping for our attention. But we can be sure of one thing: God will never give any one of us a word that is contrary to the Bible. You can be absolutely guaranteed that God will never tell you to commit adultery, or live with someone you are not married to, or marry an unbeliever. There are some things we don't need to pray about, because God has already given us the directions. As you study His Book, you will become more and more familiar with His voice, and you will learn to know when it is God speaking to you.

Read Psalm 46:10

It is really hard for some of us to sit still, but this is a discipline that we all need. Most of the time, we don't hear God's voice simply because we are so busy rushing around that we never even listen for it. We are never sitting still long enough to get an answer. God doesn't shout after us. He expects us to pull up a chair and listen.

9. What techniques can you think of that might help with listening? What can you do to keep your mind from wandering?

Lift It Up

Listening is especially hard for us, because many times we don't really want to hear God's voice. We are too busy, or we don't want to stop pursuing our own pleasures in order to sit still to hear Him. Sometimes we hear the voice of God, but we ignore it. We hear Him telling us to do something that seems too hard, and we think that if we pretend we didn't hear, we won't be held accountable. But God won't let us get away with this. He never lets us sidestep issues. He holds us smack in the middle of our issues until we sit down, listen, and take steps to obey His direction.

Let's begin one of the greatest adventures of life. As you open up to transparent prayer, you will experience God's peace and power. Don't be shy about it. Reflect, open up your heart to God, listen to Him, praise Him, and watch your life change. Come on out into the deep water!

10. In your prayer life, a few small tweaks can help you dive so much deeper. What are some tweaks you have discovered that you need to make?

11. Is there anything you feel the need to pour your heart out to God about? How can this group join you in praying for this situation?

Take time to pray together, opening up your heart so you can discover the adventures of prayer together.

My Prayer Needs:

My Group's Prayer Needs:

before session three

DEVOTIONALS

Day 1: Philippians 4:6

Do not be anxious about anything, but in everything, by prayer and petition, with thanksgiving, present your requests to God.

God wants to give to us, but He also wants us to ask Him for what we need. Sometimes we may wonder why God doesn't just automatically provide for us everything we might need. After all, if He knows everything, surely He knows when we are in trouble, when we need healing, and when we need discipline.

God does know all our needs, both physical and spiritual, but He also wants us to realize that we are not self-sufficient, that only He can provide what we need. If He automatically fulfilled our every want, we would forget where it all comes from. We would forget to whom we owe everything good. Think about the rain as an example: God said that He would send the rain to fall on the just and the unjust alike. It is a blessing that He gives to the earth because we need it, and He didn't wait for us to ask for it. But how long has it been since you thanked God for rain? Do you remember all the things He gives us just because He knows we need them? God wants us to ask Him for what we need because He wants a relationship with us.

Make a list of the "forgotten blessings" of your life. Take time to thank God specifically for these good things, making your requests "with thanksgiving."

Healing

Day 2: Acts 9:40-41

Peter sent them all out of the room; then he got down on his knees and prayed. Turning toward the dead woman, he said, "Tabitha, get up." She opened her eyes, and seeing Peter she sat up. He took her by the hand and helped her to her feet. Then he called the believers and the widows and presented her to them alive.

Hardly anything is more exciting than a miraculous answer to prayer. Tabitha (also called Dorcas) was a much-loved disciple living in Joppa. She was well known for her loving and giving spirit; she is described as "always doing good and helping the poor." When she got sick and died rather suddenly, the other believers asked Peter to come and comfort them. He arrived to find the house crowded with people she had helped, weeping for her death. Then Peter did the thing that we are often too timid to do. He asked God for a miracle. God said, "Yes," and Tabitha was raised to life again. It must have been unbelievable for those who had been grieving just a few moments before. Peter had boldly asked God to act, and there there she was alive again!

God is still powerful today. Do you ask Him for "big things" or do you feel too timid?

Little & big G.D. all kinds of things [illegible] living, seeing it

Day 3: Acts 4:29-31

"Now, Lord, consider their threats and enable your servants to speak your word with great boldness. Stretch out your hand to heal and perform miraculous signs and wonders through the name of your holy servant Jesus." After they prayed, the place where they were meeting was shaken. And they were all filled with the Holy Spirit and spoke the word of God boldly.

When we hear about the prayers of the Christians in Acts, and see the way that God answered them, it sounds thrilling. The problem is, we don't always get these answers ourselves. In fact, it seems at times that God isn't even listening. We ask Him for the things we think we need, and there is no answer. Why would this be? Is God just playing with us? When we are struggling with the problem of unanswered prayer, we have one important thing to learn: God doesn't necessarily answer the way that we want Him to. He doesn't always grant miracles; He seldom speaks audibly to us. But we can be assured that He will answer, and that He will answer in the best way at the best time.

Read Psalm 86:5-10. God didn't always say "Yes" to David either, but look at what David had to say about God's character.

Day 4: Romans 11:33-36

Oh, the depth of the riches of the wisdom and knowledge of God! How unsearchable his judgments, and his paths beyond tracing out! Who has known the mind of the Lord? Or who has been his counselor? Who has ever given to God that God should repay him? For from him and through him and to him are all things. To him be the glory forever! Amen.

When God doesn't seem to answer, or when He gives a "No" for something we are sure should have been a "Yes," it can be hard to know how to respond. Sometimes, it is tempting to be frustrated with God. We grow discouraged or even quit praying. As humans, we are often so sure that we know the best answer to our situation that we tell God exactly what we want Him to do, and then we are upset when He doesn't do it our way. We must learn that God's ways are different from ours. He actually has all the information; He can see the whole picture. His wisdom is beyond anything that we can understand, and He will always do the best thing. It is our job to stop trying to tell God exactly how to handle each situation, and leave the outcome in His hands. Ask Him, and then leave the answer to Him.

What is a situation in your life where you are trying to dictate how God should answer? Write out a prayer asking God to open your heart to His plans.

Day 5: 2 Corinthians 12:7-9

To keep me from becoming conceited because of these surpassing great revelations, there was given me a thorn in my flesh, a messenger of Satan, to torment me. Three times I pleaded with the Lord to take it away from me. But he said to me, "My grace is sufficient for you, for my power is made perfect in weakness." Therefore I will boast all the more gladly about my weaknesses, so that Christ's power may rest on me.

The Apostle Paul was a man used by God in an amazing way. From being a Christ-hater and persecutor of believers, God's grace changed Paul into a great preacher and missionary, and the author of 13 books of the New Testament. At some point in his ministry, Paul began to have trouble with what he called his "thorn in the flesh." No one knows exactly what this was. .But, it was clearly a problem; something that made life difficult for him.

Nothing could seem simpler than asking God to take away a problem that made life and ministry a struggle. Surely, Paul's request was for a good thing, and surely God would not withhold such a good thing from him. Yet, that is just what God did. He answered with "No," instead of the "Yes" that Paul hoped for. Paul saw the reasoning clearly. Because of this weakness, Paul would never forget to whom he owed his strength. He could never think that he did great things for God because he himself was especially wonderful. God would always have to be in the forefront.

Look at the problems you have in your life now. How could God be glorified by these difficulties you have? How could this perspective change the way you look at your problems?

coping c problems, strength etc

Day 6: 2 Timothy 2:13; Hebrews 10:23

If we are faithless, he will remain faithful, for he cannot disown himself.

Let us hold unswervingly to the hope we profess, for he who promised is faithful.

God has given us many promises. He promised that He would never leave us or forsake us. He promised that if we gave our lives to Him, He would keep us safe and bring us into His presence in the end. He promised that He would listen when we talked to Him, and that He would make us like His Son. We know that He will follow through on His promises, because God is faithful. It would be impossible for God to lie to us, or to fail in what He sets out to do.

In light of this, every time we see what appears to be an unanswered prayer, we can always fall back on the knowledge of God's faithfulness. He will surely fulfill His promises in the end. He is wholly trustworthy. He is not missing what is going on in our lives.

Read Deuteronomy 7:9. Write it down and put it somewhere prominent and visible as a constant reminder of God's faithfulness. Memorize this verse.

Day 7: Hebrews 11:36-39

Some faced jeers and flogging, while still others were chained and put in prison. They were stoned; they were sawed in two; they were put to death by the sword. They went about in sheepskins and goatskins, destitute, persecuted and mistreated—the world was not worthy of them. They wandered in deserts and mountains, and in caves and holes in the ground. These were all commended for their faith, yet none of them received what had been promised.

In some ways, the hardest of all God's answers is "Wait." When He answers "Yes," it is thrilling and exciting. At least with the answer "No" there is some closure—it is final. But waiting is hard for us humans. We don't like to wait; we become impatient or discouraged.

To encourage us, the Bible gives us many examples of people who were waiting for the fulfillment of God's great promise of the coming Messiah, the Savior of the world. They waited their whole lives. Many of them died terrible deaths. The prophets, who had been given God's words, were the outcasts of society. Not one of these people lived to see the promise fulfilled. God's "Wait" meant to the point of death for these people. Yet, they did not give up. Instead of being angry that they had to wait, they took God's promise as a thread of hope, and clung to it throughout all the persecution. Because they knew God was faithful, they knew that one day the promise would be fulfilled. They might never have seen it, but that part didn't matter so much as long as they were doing God's work and experiencing His presence.

What is God saying "Wait" to you about now? Are you feeling impatient, or do you see His hand in this?

Day 8: Hebrews 11:40

God had planned something better for us so that only together with us would they be made perfect.

The people mentioned in the previous verses of Hebrews 11 were faithful to the end. They believed God and served Him through persecution, rejection, and death, and yet they did not see the promise of a Savior of the world fulfilled. Why did God do this to them? Why didn't He reward their faithfulness? Why did He make them wait?

It all goes back to the fact that God sees the whole picture. He knows all the "what ifs" and "would have beens," and He plans the best possible scenario.

Looking back through your life, recount the times when you can now see that "God had planned something better."

God – money – [illegible]

Day 9: Galatians 4:4-5

But when the time had fully come, God sent his Son, born of a woman, born under law, to redeem those under law, that we might receive the full rights of sons.

Did you notice these words? "When the time had fully come." God didn't just send Jesus when He got around to it. He didn't wait until people were more worthy of being saved. He didn't wait because He was playing around with the people who were believing Him and eagerly looking for the Messiah. He waited until the best time, the optimum time, for fulfilling the prophecies and accomplishing His purposes.

During the time of the early church, most of the known world was unified under the Romans. Travel was relatively easy because of the Roman roads and the stable Roman government. The Greek Empire, which preceded Roman domination, had made the Greek language a universal second language for all educated people. The New Testament writers made use of this, writing a book that was basically understandable by anyone who was interested in its message. The Greek philosophers, with their unanswered questions about the purpose of life and the nature of God, had prepared Gentile thinkers for the acceptance of the gospel message. Jesus Christ came into the world at the perfect time, with everything arranged for the swift spread of the good news of God's salvation that is available to everyone.

God's timing can be hard to understand. Are you prepared to wait and be faithful, even though you may not ever see the results of your prayers?

Yes!

Day 10: Luke 11:11-13

"Which of you fathers, if your son asks for a fish, will give him a snake instead? Or if he asks for an egg, will give him a scorpion? If you then, though you are evil, know how to give good gifts to your children, how much more will your Father in heaven give the Holy Spirit to those who ask him!"

Even though we are sinful humans, we all have a very good idea of what a good father is like. A good father loves to give gifts to his children. When his child comes to him and says, "Please, Daddy," he enjoys fulfilling the wishes and needs of his little ones. He would never trick his children, giving them something harmful or nasty. He would always have their best in mind.

God is our very good and perfect Father. He loves to give gifts to His children, but He will only give good gifts. If your child asked you for something evil or harmful, would you give it to him? Of course not! You would want to give only good gifts to your children. That is why God doesn't always say "Yes." Sometimes He says "No," and sometimes He says "Not just yet."

When you pray and ask God for the things you desire and need, do you remember to say, "If this is Your will"? God will only give us the best, at the best time. Ask Him for wisdom in your wanting. Ask Him to conform your will to His.

1-14

session three

SMALL-GROUP SESSION

A Bad Prayer Day: Responding to Unanswered Prayer

Hebrews 4:13; 11:39-40; Proverbs 2:8; Isaiah 55:8-9; 46:10; Matthew 5:23-24

Job was a man who endured a massive amount of turmoil. He was stripped of his possessions, his family, and his health. His friends spent all their time explaining to him that he deserved all this trouble because of what a bad guy he was. To make matters worse, it seemed that God had completely deserted him. In despair, Job complained, "I cry out to you, O God, but you do not answer; I stand up, but you merely look at me" (Job 30:20). Can you relate to that feeling? God instructs us to pray about everything, at anytime, and anywhere. Then the Bible assures us over and over that God will answer our prayers. And yet, we all know the sad storyline: we desperately need God to act, we pray, we pray more and more fervently, and nothing happens. We don't get what we asked for. Jesus said, "Ask and it will be given to you" (Matthew 7:7), but we don't get a thing! What is wrong? Is this false advertising? Was God just kidding? No, the problem is ... most of us just don't understand the way God answers prayer.

Start It Up

Wanting things is something we humans are particularly good at. We were created to be innovative, to conceptualize ideas, to desire their development, and to put them into action. The problem is that sometimes our ideas stink!

1. What is one thing you wanted desperately when you were a child? Who did you ask for it? Did you get it?

2. Looking back on it now, would you say it was good, bad, or neutral that you did (or didn't) get what you wanted?

Talk It Up

When we think about God answering prayer, most of us think in terms of miraculous "Yes" answers. We think that if we have enough faith, and pray intently for the things we want, then we will get them. That job or promotion will be ours. Our house will sell soon. Our loved one will be healed. Whatever we want will happen miraculously. We need to stop and realize that this thinking assumes a limited view of God. It puts Him in a box instead of understanding that God is almighty, all-wise, and fully in control of all He created. Sometimes our God does answer with a "Yes!" and it is thrilling when He does. Sometimes God answers with a "Wait." We don't like that response because it is hard to wait. We wonder whether God even heard us. Sometimes God answers with a "No." We wonder how could God answer "No" to this good thing we asked for? How could a loving God refuse the requests of people that matter to Him?

God Sees the Big Picture

Read Hebrews 4:13 and Proverbs 2:8

Briefly put, God says "No" when He has a better vantage point to make a decision. When we ask for something, God does not refuse our request because He doesn't want us to have a good thing. He refuses because He knows that it wouldn't be the best thing. Let's consider driving on a crowded highway during rush hour. Traffic is backed up for miles, and your lane is moving at a snail's pace. As you consider whether or not to take a different route, you are not a bit interested in the opinion of that driver in the car next to you. You want to hear what the guy in the helicopter has to say as he gives the traffic report over the radio. He is the one with the perspective, the one who can look up ahead and back behind you. When we pray we must remember that God is like the guy in the helicopter, able to see the entire freeway system of our lives. We have to trust that when God says "No" it is because He has a better outlook and He is guiding us.

God doesn't just guard and protect us from outside harm. Often, He protects us from our own foolishness. Just as a wise parent does not give a two-year-old everything she wants, God does not give us everything we want. We should thank God for His denied requests in our lives.

3. Since God sometimes does say "No," what does the promise in Luke 11:9-10 mean when it says, "Ask and it will be given you"?

God Has the Master Plan

Read Isaiah 55:8-9 and Hebrews 11:39-40

God also says "No" when He has a superior plan. We like to get down on our knees and pray, "Here is my agenda, God. Please rubber stamp it." We have things inside out. When we pray, we should exchange our outline for God's. We should come into prayer saying, "Show me what you want me to do." When we look at God's agenda, we don't always like it. His ways require endurance and courage. To follow Him will cost us something. We might have to end a relationship, or stop doing something that we like to do. We prefer our own plans because they are usually easier and meet our view of what we need. Even so, God's plan always has something better for us.

4. How should we approach planning for the future? Should we make plans at all? Check out James 4:13-15 for some ideas.

God is Moving and Shaking

Read Isaiah 46:10

God also says "No" when He has a greater outcome in store than we do. Behind every problem, there is a purpose. For some reason human beings think God owes them an explanation for His actions. We think God needs to sit down with us, pull out His appointment book, and work things out with us. But we don't deserve any such consideration. God is God, and we are not. He doesn't have to check with us before He sets His plans. We are merely sinners brought by grace into a relationship with God. If God did explain all of His actions to us, we couldn't understand most of them anyway. We are finite, He is infinite. We are limited, He is unlimited. All we can do is trust in His goodness.

Perhaps God is saying "No" to you right now. Have you considered the fact that God has a greater outcome? When God says "No," remember that His motivation is always love. The moment God says "No," the Evil One steps in and says, "Psst, God cannot be depended upon. He just loves to frustrate you." When we hear this lie, we must remember God's character. God is love. He is perfect in every way. He will always do the best thing for all concerned. On top of that, He will give us the grace we need to ride out whatever comes. The life of the Apostle Paul illustrates this well. He had some kind of physical problem that he referred to as his "thorn in the flesh." Three times, Paul prayed that God would remove it, and when God said "No" for the third time, His only answer was, "My grace is sufficient for you, for my power is made perfect in weakness" (2 Corinthians 12:9). Because of God's grace, Paul could actually rejoice in his struggles, knowing that it was for the glory of God.

5. **How have you experienced the fact that God is loving, just, and will do the best thing?**

God Keeps Us From Trouble

Sometimes God says "No," because what we are asking for is wrong. It is not simply because we don't have His perspective, or because God has a better plan. Sometimes we just make inappropriate requests. We aren't asking for a good thing, we are asking for a bad thing. God will not give us a "Yes" answer to an inappropriate prayer.

We will receive no satisfaction at all from God when we are praying for guidance about something that He has already clearly spelled out in Scripture. A prayer asking for a new and different answer will always get a "No." Don't ask Him questions when you already know the answer. If you are praying about whether to move in with your boyfriend or girlfriend, whether to marry an unbeliever, whether it is all right to cheat in this business deal, whether you should enter into an adulterous relationship, you are asking inappropriately. God has already answered, and He won't change His Word just for you.

6. What are some inappropriate prayers we pray?

God Sets His Clock Differently

God might also say "No" to us because our timing is off. God may answer our prayers later in order to answer them better. Mary and Martha sent an urgent message to Jesus one day, telling Him that their brother Lazarus was dying. Scripture records an odd response. "Jesus loved Martha and her sister and Lazarus. Yet when he heard that Lazarus was sick, he stayed where he was two more days" (John 11:5-6). He loved them, but He didn't answer right away. How could He do such a thing? Why didn't He rush to Lazarus' side, heal him, and spare Mary and Martha the pain of his illness and death? Instead of responding immediately, Jesus waited where He was until Lazarus died. He didn't answer Mary and Martha. He just waited. Finally, after Lazarus was dead, Jesus got up to go see him. Instead of healing Lazarus on his sickbed, Jesus called him out of his tomb. This story begs the question, "Which was the greater miracle? Which was the greater witness?" The sisters could not have known that their timing was off. They were not out of line to ask Jesus for help. When we pray appropriately and with proper motives, and still seem to get no answer, we must remember Lazarus and his sisters. Sometimes God's answer is simply "Wait." Could your timing be off?

7. In your everyday life, what is one thing you hate to wait on? How do you react?

8. How do you react when you have to wait on God?

God Plugs His Ears

There are times when we get no answer from God because we have a sin problem. If we have unconfessed, living sin in our lives, God is not going to answer our prayers. Essentially, He will plug His ears and not attend to our requests. God is holy and He cannot let us skip over ongoing, pet sins and just move on as if everything is okay. God's response is to camp out right on top of our sin issues until we are ready to come to grips with confession and repentance. Every time we try to move on ... every time we try to ask about something else ... every time we change the subject, He is going to say, "No way. Come deal with this ugly sin first." We may complain that this "little sin" has nothing to do with the issue at hand, but God won't change. We must deal with unconfessed sin before we can expect answered prayers.

Another problem we may have is unresolved relational conflict. If we hold grudges, have refused to forgive or apologize, or have offended someone, then our prayers will be hindered.

Read Matthew 5:23-24

9. Why does God require us to resolve our conflicts with other people in order to keep our prayer connection with Him?

Lift It Up

Unanswered prayer may seem like a mystery, but when we look at it from God's perspective, realizing that He can see the whole picture, it makes more sense. We must learn to trust in His love, and realize that His plan is bigger and better, fitting in all the puzzling pieces. We should examine our own motives so we pray prayers that honor God and don't promote selfish interests. As we examine our own hearts, we will know if we are harboring sins that would hinder our prayers. As we examine our relationships with other people, we can deal with bitterness, unforgiveness, and pride. Having a perspective of the various reasons God might respond negatively to our prayers, allows us to deal with it in faith and obedience to God, enabling us to become true men and women of prayer.

10. What is a prayer that you are waiting to have answered? How has this study helped you understand why you don't have an answer yet?

Take time to pray together, asking God to reveal things that may be hindering your prayer life.

My Prayer Needs:

My Group's Prayer Needs:

Bea - Nancy A. + Eddie great neph
Nan - Jacob grandson need life - niece Jack Wilson
Linda - no
Sam - no
Sis - Jennifer [illegible], Luke gr. son,
Birdwomen - [illegible]
Joyce - no
June - [illegible], Charlie - [illegible] Bonnie Bart [illegible]
Charlie - } [illegible]
Cheno -
Sheryl - aunt (90 uncle) needs help - al & 3 kids
West Virg. + moving

B
S
M
C
C
J
Nancy

before session four

DEVOTIONALS

Day 1: 1 Thessalonians 4:3a,7

It is God's will that you should be sanctified ... For God did not call us to be impure, but to live a holy life.

We talk a lot about wanting "God's will for my life." It sounds romantic and mysterious and holy, and we imagine that if only we had this elusive instruction book all our problems would be solved. While it is true that God will guide us throughout our lives in very specific ways, He has already told us exactly what His "will for our lives" is: that we should be sanctified. That means He wants us to become holy; to be different than we were before we knew Him. He wants us to become like His Son. He wants to clean out all the corners of our hearts and make us clean and pure before Him.

As always, God leaves part of this in our hands. If He is going to change us, we have to yield to Him. We have to come to Him and say, "Clean me. Change me. Transform me—even if it hurts."

What is an area that you are holding on to that you need to yield to God?

Day 2: Ephesians 3:17b-19

And I pray that you, being rooted and established in love, may have power, together with all the saints, to grasp how wide and long and high and deep is the love of Christ, and to know this love that surpasses knowledge—that you may be filled to the measure of all the fullness of God.

Wide and long and high and deep—the love of Christ is bigger than we can ever imagine. We can see the words, but grasping the reality is another matter. In fact, there is really only one way, and that is to experience it. Think about a big lake. You can see that it is wide and long. You can even get into a boat and row across it to get a good picture of its size. You can measure how deep it is with a string and a weight. You can take its temperature, and study the plants along its edges. You can talk about it and think about it and dream about it without ever getting your big toe wet. But as long as you are staying dry, you have missed the essence of this lake. You are not going to fully grasp it until you are out over your head in the water.

The love of Christ is like this. We can talk about it, and look at it, and stay nice and dry in the boat, but until we jump overboard nd get out over our heads, we are not going to grasp how "wide and long and high and deep is the love of Christ." It surpasses knowledge; it requires experience.

Are you ready to risk leaving the boat, and learn about Christ's love by experience? Are you ready to be open and vulnerable, to let Him change you even when it hurts, to do things His way instead of your way?

Day 3: Psalm 26:2

Test me, O LORD, and try me, examine my heart and my mind; for your love is ever before me, and I walk continually in your truth.

The prophet Jeremiah said, "The heart is deceitful above all things and beyond cure. Who can understand it?" (Jeremiah 17:9). We know what it means to deceive and manipulate others, but many of us don't realize that we can deceive and manipulate ourselves as well. We think that we know ourselves— that we know our own motives and thoughts—but in fact we hide from ourselves. Self-deceit is one of the ways that humans deal with sin. We pretend that it never happened, and before long we believe ourselves. In order to have real victory in life—in order to be doing God's will and to be sanctified—we need help. We don't even know half the sins that we have in our own hearts. We need to ask God to open our hearts, and show us the things that are hiding in the dark corners.

It will be hard to pray this kind of prayer—most of the time, we would rather not know what our hearts are really like. The good news is that God won't show us everything at once. Instead, He shows us just a few things, and helps us deal with them a little at a time.

Pray and ask God to show you the things that are hiding in the dark corners of your heart.

Day 4: 2 Corinthians 13:5-6

Examine yourselves to see whether you are in the faith; test yourselves. Do you not realize that Christ Jesus is in you—unless, of course, you fail the test? And I trust that you will discover that we have not failed the test.

Part of sanctification—becoming more and more like Christ—is learning to examine ourselves. When we ask God to examine us, it is like we are asking Him to shine His spotlight on our hearts. As we read and understand more and more of His Word, we will find that it is like a handheld spotlight that we can use on ourselves. God wants us to apply what we read, to shine the light on ourselves, and look at who we really are without flinching. We are not allowed to just lay in our spiritual hammocks and rest, ignoring the bad parts of our lives. If we are really Christ followers, one of the things we will see when we shine that light on ourselves is Jesus working in our lives. Because of this, self-examination is encouraging as well as painful. God doesn't expect us to become holy by our own efforts. He is doing that work in our lives as we give Him access.

A certain amount of introspection is valuable for learning who we really are before God, but it is only valuable if it is coupled with Scripture reading. Are you prone to just being introspective? Or, are you also applying God's Word to your life?

Day 5: Psalm 51:16-17

You do not delight in sacrifice, or I would bring it; you do not take pleasure in burnt offerings. The sacrifices of God are a broken spirit; a broken and contrite heart, O God, you will not despise.

When we have been examined, we are surely going to find some problems in our lives. No one is without fault. Some problems will be painful; some embarrassing; some surprising; and some very, very hard to get rid of. What should we do about these things when God brings them to our attention?

For an answer, look at the life of David. He committed some really serious sins. First, he stole another man's wife. Then, to cover it up, he murdered her husband, his loyal friend. When God confronted David with his sin, David responded the right way. He was heart-broken to realize how far he had strayed from God's ways. He wept and pleaded with God for forgiveness. He turned from his sin; he did not try to excuse himself, or minimize what he had done.

It is hard on our pride to respond with brokenness. We want to justify what we've done, to explain how it really wasn't that bad, or how we couldn't help it, or that it was someone else's fault. But, none of this is works for God. Only a "broken and contrite" heart realizes the full enormity of sin, and grasps its real need for God.

It might seem frightening to be humble and broken; it is a very vulnerable position. But God is merciful. Choose one of these verses, write it down on a card, and memorize this week:

> **Psalm 147:3 – He heals the brokenhearted and binds up their wounds.**
>
> **Psalm 34:18 – The LORD is close to the brokenhearted and saves those who are crushed in spirit.**

Day 6: Isaiah 48:10-11

See, I have refined you, though not as silver; I have tested you in the furnace of affliction. For my own sake, for my own sake, I do this. How can I let myself be defamed? I will not yield my glory to another.

In some parts of the world, the river sand is full of gold dust. It is free for the taking, all you have to do is pick it up. This sounds simple, but collecting gold from the bottom of a river is hard work. Even when the dust and sand have been separated, the gold is mixed with dirt and other impurities. It does not look pretty. It can't be made into coins or jewelry. Only an expert would guess that any gold is there. Before the gold has any real value, it must be refined. The impurities must be burned out or skimmed off, and the real gold melted and collected together. In ancient times, the purest gold was refined seven times in a hot fire. Some say that the ultimate test of purity was for the gold to be so clear and smooth that the refiner could see his own reflection in the molten metal.

We are like the unrefined gold—mixed with dirt and impurities. Only God can see the real gold mixed in. In order to make us beautiful and useful, God has to refine us. The trials and temptations that we undergo in life are like the fire that the refiner uses to melt the gold and remove the impurities. It is painful to be refined. No one enjoys being in the fire, but we can rejoice nevertheless when we realize what God is using the fire for.

Read 1 Peter 1:6-7. Have you turned yourself over to God to be refined? What trials do you have in your life right now? How do you think God might be using them for your benefit?

Day 7: Acts 8:26-27b

Now an angel of the Lord said to Philip, "Go south to the road—the desert road—that goes down from Jerusalem to Gaza." So he started out ...

God's will for our lives is the simplest and yet the hardest thing in the world: He wants us to look like Jesus. This is God's will in its overwhelming completeness. At the same time, God also desires to work His will in us as He guides us through life. Even the smallest decisions can have far-reaching consequences. If your heart is open to God's leading, your life will be open to some of the most thrilling experiences possible.

Make it a habit, as you plan what you are doing, to ask God what He wants you to do. Ask Him for specific guidance, and tell Him you are willing to change your plans to fit His. Philip was a man who was open to the leading of the Holy Spirit. He was not wrapped up in his own agenda, but had his ear tuned to God's voice. When the Lord sent Philip the message to go, Philip didn't ask any questions. He just simply got up and went. As a result, God used him to explain the good news to a traveler with a seeking heart. The man was baptized and "went on his way rejoicing" (Acts 8:39). Because of Philip's obedience and openness, a man came to know Christ, and the good news of the gospel was presumably carried over into Africa.

Being guided by God means being in line for great blessing. Have you consciously prayed for His leading, and then taken the time to really listen?

Day 8: Isaiah 6:8

Then I heard the voice of the LORD saying, "Whom shall I send? And who will go for us?" And I said, "Here am I. Send me!"

Do you long to experience God in a greater way? Do you ever feel dissatisfied with your relationship with Him, and wish for something tangible, something thrilling to happen? If you are feeling this way, ask yourself this question: "Have I ever turned my life over to God, and said, 'Use me!'?" Many times, if we honestly look at our hearts, we will find that we have been keeping at least one little comfort zone back for ourselves. We don't want to do anything too hard, or give up any nice thing that we enjoy. We think that if we offer ourselves and our resources to God, He will take it all, and we will have nothing. That is true; He will take it all. But He will give back more than we have ever dreamed of. This life holds nothing better than being an effective tool in the hands of our Maker.

Read Jeremiah 1:4-10. We may feel unworthy, unequipped and frightened. But remember, God is doing the work, not us. We just have the joy and privilege of participating.

Day 9: Luke 18:22

When Jesus heard this, he said to him, "You still lack one thing. Sell everything you have and give to the poor, and you will have treasure in heaven. Then come, follow me."

One day a very wealthy young man came to Jesus. He was an upright citizen, influential, a public official, and he was attracted to Jesus' teachings. "What must I do to be saved?" he asked. In reply Jesus said, "You know the commandments." He quoted some of the 10 that God gave Moses on the mountain, and the young man said, "I do all that." He was probably saying to himself, "This is easier than I thought." Then Jesus did the thing that God does so often. He did not leave him standing there thinking he had everything sewed up. Instead, Jesus stretched him. He pinpointed that one area of his life that the young man did not want to turn over to God. Jesus told him to give away all of his money. If he really wanted to be saved, he would have to trade his earthly treasure for treasure in heaven. He would have to follow Jesus.

Over and over again as you progress in your journey of faith, you are going to find that God will stretch you. As soon as you start to think that you have made it, that you now no longer have to struggle with sin, that you really understand all doctrine, or that God's ways are an open book to you, He will stretch you some more. His ways are not our ways, He will constantly surprise us by stepping out of the box we make for Him. Are you willing to grow, to learn to be more like Him? It takes a lot of stretching, but it will be worth it. Don't be like the rich young man who turned away because he thought Jesus asked for too much.

In what ways has God stretched you recently? Write some of these down. Did you recognize this as stretching at the time, or were you just annoyed?

Day 10: Philippians 3:8

What is more, I consider everything a loss compared to the surpassing greatness of knowing Christ Jesus my Lord, for whose sake I have lost all things. I consider them rubbish, that I may gain Christ ...

In life, we have such a hard time stepping out of our nice, comfortable, dry boat. We don't want to get wet. We are afraid that we might lose something that we don't want to lose. We become so attached to the status quo that we become blinded to heaven. Don't miss the best things. Listen to Paul's words. Everything that he had before—prestige, education, family background, possessions, security, everything—was worthless to him when compared to Christ. When we experience how "wide and deep and high and long is the love of Christ," we won't be looking back.

Have you stepped out of the boat this week? Write down the things you prayed for, and be sure to leave a place to write down what happens as a result.

session four

SMALL-GROUP SESSION

For Mature Audiences Only: Exploring the Depths of Prayer

Psalm 139; James 1:3-4

To many of us, the idea of praying seriously makes us feel like we are in an inflatable boat, floating over shark-infested waters. We cling with white knuckles to the sides of the craft and remain in the protective environment that we are familiar with. We don't want to go overboard into the deep waters, and we don't want to test out the unknown. It's frightening to be that vulnerable. We need someone to knock us out of the boat and let us experience the power of deep-water, dangerous prayer.

Start It Up

Some people love water so much they seem to have fins, but some of us are just waders.

1. **How old were you when you learned to swim? Do you like deep water, or would you rather stay in the wading pool?**

2. How do you feel about other kinds of risks and dangers? Are you more likely to take physical risks or emotional/relational risks?

Talk It Up

The Bible is full of dozens and dozens of deep-water prayers. In this session, we are going to spotlight six of these prayers. We will label each one with a two-word sound bite to help us remember them and begin to use them as models for our prayers.

"Examine Me"

Read Psalm 139

The first deep-water, dangerous prayer is "examine me." In an operating room, the doctors use the brightest lights possible to illuminate the area they are working on. When we ask God to examine us, we are asking Him to turn on the spotlight of His brilliant holiness and let it shine into the inner recesses of our souls. David's psalm is a good example of an "examine me" prayer. He starts the prayer by praising God for His omniscience—all-knowing nature. Then he praises God for His omnipresence—ever-present nature. He praises God for His omnipotence—all-powerful nature. After he praises God, David begins to express his anger at the wicked who flagrantly disobey God. Then, as he looks at the wicked in God's spotlight, David requests, "Can you turn your spotlight on me God? Where do I fall short? Where am I, like these wicked people, offensive to You?" Most of us don't have the courage to pray this prayer. We would rather stand in the shadows, not too close to that penetrating bright light. If it is a little dark, our dirt doesn't show much.

Are you willing to muster up the courage to pray this prayer? There is no telling what God's light will expose. It may be painful, but if you follow through, and deal with what He exposes, you will become the man or woman that God wants you to be for this generation.

3. Once you have prayed "examine me," what should you do with what God shows you? What can happen if God shows you something that is wrong in your life and you continue to ignore it?

"Break Me"

The second deep-water prayer is "break me." If you pray the first prayer, "God, expose whatever it is that is keeping me from you, then you have to pray the "break me" prayer. What has leeched onto you? What behavioral pattern needs to be broken and extracted? What does God need to do to deal with the cancerous growths He exposed in your life? Will you allow Him to take care of it, and to cut it out of your life? Over and over in the Gospels, we see Jesus healing people, casting out demons, and forgiving sins. In many instances, He leaves the people He helps with the words, "Go and sin no more." With God's help, you too must break those destructive, sin-driven behavioral patterns, because they are destroying your life and the lives of others. Once you become a "new creature" in Christ, you have the opportunity to develop totally new patterns of thought and action.

Read what happens to Zacchaeus in Luke 19. Zacchaeus is a tax collector, a dishonest man who regularly steals from his fellow Jews, making himself rich as a result. He is a thief and a traitor to his people. He might have kept on that way if Zacchaeus had not met Jesus Christ. After the meal that he shares with the Lord, Zacchaeus comes out of his house announcing that he is giving back all the money he has stolen—multiplied by four. Because of his contact with Jesus, Zacchaeus breaks and extracts the behavioral patterns that have been ruining his life.

It is tough to pray a "break me" prayer. It hurts to break. We are afraid of the pain, but we should be more afraid of the pain we will have if we don't change the destructive patterns of the past. What needs to be broken in your life? What is keeping you from the abundant life Jesus offers? Could it be lust? Could it be anger? Could it be selfishness? Could it be materialism? As God exposes your sin, let your next prayer be "God, break me."

4. When you pray "break me," what is your responsibility in the process? Are you supposed to sit back and wait for God to act, or is there something you should do? If so, what?

"Test Me"

Read James 1:3-4

The third deep-water prayer is "test me." God never tempts, but He does test us, with the goal of bringing out the best. When God tests us, He tests to build character, especially those qualities that we cannot build in ourselves.

Sometimes God tests us through a blessing. A person or family may be barely getting by financially, living month to month. Yet they are faithful with their treasures, faithful with their talents, and faithful with their time. Suddenly, God tests them by blessing them, maybe with a financial windfall, maybe with another opportunity. Sadly, in tests of blessing, people often cease to lean on God. They stop putting Him first. They begin to feel self-sufficient. They stop giving financially, and they become too busy to give of their time.

God also tests us in difficult circumstances. He doesn't make bad things happen to us, but He doesn't always protect us from the fallen, sin-infested world we live in, or from our own folly.

5. How can we recognize a test from God when we see it? What is the difference between testing and the normal problems we face in everyday life?

"Guide Me"

The fourth deep-water prayer we need to learn is "guide me." Do you really let God guide you and lead you in all aspects of your life? A "guide me" prayer may feel like a dangerous prayer, but it is even more dangerous to blunder through life without ever asking God what He wants you to be doing. When you don't ask God for direction, when you are not living your life looking for what He wants you to do, then you are missing out on the best that God has planned for you. We have no idea what God wants to do through ordinary people like us. As you seek His will and follow His guidance, amazing things could happen!

6. **In what ways does God guide? Since He usually doesn't speak audibly, or send us step-by-step instruction manuals in the mail, how can we learn to recognize His guidance?**

"Use Me"

The fifth prayer is "use me." When you pray a "use me" prayer, you are saying, "God, here is everything: my talents, my abilities, my achievements, my creativity, my resources. It all comes from You, God. I'm giving it all back to you. Use me." Even though we are imperfect, saved by grace sinners, God will link us up with someone who needs what we have to offer. When God uses us in even a small way, there is nothing like it. It never gets old, it never gets stale, it never ever gets boring. The sad thing is that many of us miss this joy because we never turn to God and say, "Use me."

7. **What is a personal experience you have had (good or bad) that God could or did use to impact others?**

8. Consider the people in your group. What are some qualities in them that you could see God using for His purposes?

"Stretch Me"

The sixth deep-water prayer that we have to learn is "stretch me." The Gospel of John tells us the story of a religious leader who came to visit Jesus at night. He came through the shadows to meet Jesus one evening because he had heard that Jesus preached a different way to get to heaven. Jesus stretched Nicodemus' spiritual understanding. He said, "You must be born again."

How many of us will miss heaven because we have grown up just accepting our religious party line, thinking we will get to heaven by rules or rituals? That is not the way. The way is a person. The way becomes a part of your life when you say, "Jesus, stretch my spiritual understanding. I want to ask you to come into my life, and to take control. I want to be born again into the family of God." When you have prayed this, whether it was long ago, or just now, then you need to ask God to continue to stretch you. Ask Him to work in your marriage, your career, your money management. Ask Him to stretch your courage, and expand your vision.

9. **Even the most "open-minded" people will find out sooner or later that God's way of thinking is different from anything they have ever experienced. When has God stretched your thinking, and taught you something that "went against the grain" of your thought patterns?**

Lift It Up

This is deep-water prayer. If you jump out of your safe little boat, if you dive down deep into dangerous and painful prayers, if you stop skimming the surface and become really serious about following God, you are in line for greater blessing and greater adventure than you ever dreamed of.

10. Together, ask God for courage to pray these deep-water prayers. Is there some area of your life, or a difficult situation that needs special help? Share these needs with the group, and pray together for God's help and guidance.

11. Have you asked Jesus Christ to take control of your life, and stretch your spiritual understanding? If not, your leader would be glad to talk with you about this.

Take time to delve into some deep-water praying together.

My Prayer Needs:

My Group's Prayer Needs:

Chris – Beth Rew – Don Ryder 92 y/o Beanah... eye ... [illegible]

James – Maxine's husband – School. Bother,

Charlie – no

Hugh – no

Elsa – Gary & Pam Howell, ... [illegible]

Mary – Vivian Matthew 95 – 2 ... [illegible]

Joyce – Pat Barton ... daughter

before session five

DEVOTIONALS

Day 1: 1 Thessalonians 5:17

Pray continually.

Prayer is more than an occasional action, or even a regular practice. Prayer is a way of life. The command to "pray continually" looks impossible to us, and perhaps it is. Even if we could spend the day on our knees, instead of working and relating to people, we wouldn't be able to keep our minds on our prayers. However, we can and must cultivate an attitude and habit of continual prayer. When we understand that we build a relationship with God through prayer, it becomes more than a routine. It is communication with One we know and love well. A life that is Christ centered is going to be characterized by prayer. Every thought, every event or little trouble, or even joke, will be shared with Him. Continuous prayer isn't supposed to be a duty to struggle though. We have been given the tremendous privilege of free access to God, and told to take advantage of it.

Life is hard, we need all the help we can get. Don't neglect your greatest resource. Do you pray continuously? Do you pray regularly? Pray now and ask God to teach you how to make prayer an ongoing part of your day.

Day 2: Psalm 63:6-7

On my bed I remember you; I think of you through the watches of the night. Because you are my help, I sing in the shadow of your wings.

As you build your relationship with God through prayer, you will find that as you know Him more, you will love Him more. The more you think about Him and talk to Him, the more He will show up in all you say, do, and think. Sometimes, He might even wake you up out of your sleep to talk to you. When you lie in your bed, is your first waking thought of Him? Do you recognize His presence with you? It won't always be something you feel. God isn't very often "warm and fuzzy." But when you know Him, just recognizing that He is with you is all you need.

Many people find that night is the time to worry. We are relaxed from the busy pace of the day, and all the thoughts we have pushed aside come crowding back. Try consciously thinking of God "through the watches of the night." If you go to sleep thinking of Him, you will wake up thinking of Him too.

Day 3: Daniel 1:6,17

Among these were some [men] from Judah: Daniel, Hananiah, Mishael, and Azariah ... To these four young men God gave knowledge and understanding of all kinds of literature and learning. And Daniel could understand visions and dreams of all kinds.

Very few people will have the kind of experiences Daniel had. He was chosen by God to fill a special role in showing God's power to the Babylonians. He was very young when he was taken into captivity, but even at an early age his devotion to God was remarkable. Daniel was blessed by God with extraordinary intelligence and wisdom, and for this reason he was chosen, along with several other promising young Hebrews, to serve King Nebuchadnezzar.

Such an opportunity could have been a heady experience for a young man, but Daniel did not allow his new position to change his relationship with God. Risking the displeasure of the chief official, Daniel and his three friends determined not to defile themselves by eating any of the food God had forbidden them to eat. God blessed their efforts to remain pure in His sight, gave them health, wisdom, and favor in the eyes of their captors.

If you read the entire story of Daniel, you will see that he was a man whose life was characterized by prayer. He consistently put his relationship with God first, trusting God for the outcome.

Do you trust God to run your life, or are you still trying to hold the reins?

Day 4: Daniel 2:17-19

Then Daniel returned to his house and explained the matter to his friends Hananiah, Mishael and Azariah. He urged them to plead for mercy from the God of heaven concerning this mystery, so that he and his friends might not be executed with the rest of the wise men of Babylon. During the night the mystery was revealed to Daniel in a vision. Then Daniel praised the God of heaven.

King Nebuchadnezzar had a strange and troubling dream. He could not understand it, but he was sure that it had some deep meaning. The natural thing to do was to call up his wise men and sorcerers to ask them what the meaning of the dream might be. But Nebuchadnezzar was suspicious and crafty. He wanted to be sure that he was receiving the real interpretation, not just something the wise men invented to satisfy his curiosity, so he refused to tell the dream. He would know the interpretation was true, he said, only if the interpreter could prove his insight by accurately telling what the king had dreamed. It was a good test, and of course the wise men failed. The king was angry at having been so deceived in the value of these counselors, and determined to put all the wise men of his kingdom to death. This included Daniel and his three friends.

When Daniel heard what was planned, he knew where to turn. He knew God, and he knew that only God could give the interpretation of the king's dream and save their lives. His instant reaction was to pray and ask God for His help. Because of Daniel's faith and prayers, the dream was interpreted, their lives were saved, and God was glorified. When Nebuchadnezzar saw the power of God, he said, "Surely your God is the God of gods and the Lord of kings and a revealer of mysteries, for you were able to reveal the mystery."

Read Daniel's prayer in Daniel 2:20-23. What stands out to you?

Day 5: Daniel 5:14

I have heard that the spirit of the gods is in you and you have insight, intelligence and outstanding wisdom.

Many years had passed since Daniel had interpreted Nebuchadnezzar's dream for him. Nebuchadnezzar's son, Belshazzar was ruling then, and one evening this extravagant king ordered the gold and silver vessels from the Temple of God in Jerusalem to be brought to him. He and his wives, concubines, and guests drank from them as they were praising and worshipping their pagan gods. Belshazzar did this, knowing that the God of the Temple in Jerusalem was the true God, the God who had humbled his father Nebuchadnezzar. During this feast, a hand came out of nowhere and wrote on the wall, "MENE, MENE, TEKEL, PARSIN." Roughly translated, this would be "Counted, counted, weighed, divided." Not unnaturally, this was a frightening experience and the message was cryptic and not reassuring. Belshazzar wanted someone to tell him what it meant, but he found his wise men as useless as Nebuchadnezzar had. He could think of only one man who might be able to answer him. He had heard of Daniel's reputation.

None of us have the kind of reputation that Daniel did. We are not interpreters of dreams, or endowed with extraordinary intelligence, or prophecies of the future. Nevertheless, Belshazzar's description of Daniel can apply to every believer. Everyone who has been born again and adopted into God's family has the Spirit of God dwelling in him. The more we pray and communicate with God, the better we will know Him. The better we know God, the more "insight, intelligence and outstanding wisdom" He will give us.

In what ways have you seen the Spirit of God work in your life, giving you insight in various situations?

Day 6: Daniel 6:10

Now when Daniel learned that the decree had been published, he went home to his upstairs room where the windows opened toward Jerusalem. Three times a day he got down on his knees and prayed, giving thanks to God, just as he had done before.

Daniel had reached such a position of influence that the other wise men grew jealous, and plotted a clever way to dispose of him. They persuaded Darius the king to issue an unbreakable decree that for 30 days all prayers must be directed to the king. Anyone who prayed to any other god would be put to death by being thrown to the lions. These jealous men knew that by such a decree they would be sure to catch Daniel. His integrity and devotion to God was so well known that they were sure he would not bend.

They were right. Daniel's relationship with God was not the kind of thing that could be hidden or put aside because of fear. Daniel prayed as usual, openly and faithfully. He knew that he might die, but he trusted God. Once again, the result was victory. He was indeed thrown to the lions, but the next morning when Darius rushed to find him, he was still alive. "When Daniel was lifted from the den, no wound was found on him, because he had trusted in his God."

Could an adversary catch you in the same kind of trap that Daniel was caught in? Is prayer this important to you?

Day 7: Daniel 9:22-23

He instructed me and said to me, "Daniel, I have now come to give you insight and understanding. As soon as you began to pray, an answer was given, which I have come to tell you, for you are highly esteemed.

Can you imagine receiving this kind of answer to prayer? One of Gods chief angels showed up with an answer, saying he was highly esteemed by God ... wow! Daniel was an amazing man of prayer. He made prayer such a part of his life that he was willing to risk death rather than even appear to compromise his commitment to the one true God. From the time when he first became famous for interpreting Nebuchadnezzar's dream until the time when God gave him the visions of the future, Daniel was faithful in prayer. He put his trust in God, and as he yielded himself to God, God used him in more and more spectacular ways. It is true that not many are chosen to be prophets, or to see God work in such amazing ways as Daniel did. Nevertheless, every believer who yields to God as Daniel did, and remains faithful in prayer, will find that God uses the trusting heart in greater and greater ways.

Do you want to be used by God, and see great things happen for His kingdom? Begin by learning to pray with trust.

Day 8: Psalm 66:17-20

I cried out to him with my mouth; his praise was on my tongue. If I had cherished sin in my heart, the Lord would not have listened; but God has surely listened and heard my voice in prayer. Praise be to God, who has not rejected my prayer or withheld his love from me!

We don't like to think about sin too much. It is much nicer to talk about how God always listens to us and loves to answer our prayers, but this is not the whole picture. God does listen to us and does love to answer our prayers, but if we are harboring known sin in our hearts, He will not respond to us. God is a holy God. No sin can be in His presence. It is a barrier between us and God. Christ died in order to remove that barrier of sin, and allow us free access to God. But if we persist in hanging on to a deliberate sin, it will be a barrier that hinders our prayers.

God won't give you the answer to your next question until you have dealt with what you already know about.

Examine your heart. Is there anything that you need to confess to God in order to be able to come before Him with a clean heart? Read Psalm 24:3-5.

Day 9: Revelation 5:8

And when he had taken it, the four living creatures and the twenty-four elders fell down before the Lamb. Each one had a harp and they were holding golden bowls full of incense, which are the prayers of the saints.

When God gave Moses the instructions for building the tabernacle, and for the forms of worship, one of the things that He ordered was the burning of fragrant incense. Every morning and evening the priest was to burn incense on the altar, so that "incense will burn regularly before the LORD for the generations to come" (Exodus 30:8). Many of us don't think of burning incense in worship today, but when John had his vision of heaven and the last days, he saw incense still brought before the Lord.

The prayers of the saints (those who are Christ-followers) are like a sweet-smelling incense to God. Prayer is for communication, but it is also for worship. Our prayers honor and glorify God, and have a special place in the heavenly worship services.

Does this view of prayer give you a new feeling about its value? Are you taking time each day to offer praise and worship to God?

Day 10: Psalm 34:1-3

I will extol the LORD at all times; his praise will always be on my lips. My soul will boast in the LORD; let the afflicted hear and rejoice. Glorify the LORD with me; let us exalt his name together.

At first, the idea of continually praying may seem impossible and overwhelming. We don't know how to do it, we don't know what to say. We may not be able to think of eloquent words or important requests, but every day we can cultivate an attitude and habit of thanksgiving. No matter what else is happening, we can praise God for some good thing that He has done for us. As we learn to continually praise the Lord, to continually thank Him, we will find that we are continually praying.

We don't want to cultivate a fake "praise the Lord" that we tack onto every sentence, but rather to practice genuine praise, thanksgiving, and prayer. You might start by trying to pause three times each day to offer heartfelt thanks to God for at least one thing. Try the first one now.

session five

SMALL-GROUP SESSION

Blown Away: Getting Motivation to Pray

Exodus 17:8-16; Luke 18:1-8; Ephesians 6:10-18

If you knew beyond a shadow of a doubt that God would grant your request the moment you prayed it, what would you pray for at this moment? Some would pray, "Rebuild my marriage." Others would pray, "Give me direction." Still others would pray, "Bring back my wayward child."

Do you know that God is yearning to hear those very prayers right now? He really wants us to tell Him about all that troubles us and all that is in our hearts. He wants to comfort, lead, and guide us. As our Father, He longs for a deep and continual relationship with you and me. And He will answer our prayers. We have already learned that God is not always going to answer prayer the way we want Him to, but He will answer in the way that is best for us.

Start It Up

Communication is an integral part of being human, but sometimes we don't do it very effectively.

1. **Who do you feel listens and responds to you the best? What makes you choose this person?**

2. When you feel you have something important to communicate, would you rather talk or write? Why?

Talk It Up

In any group of Christ-followers we will find three basic stages of prayer development.

Stage 1 is made up of the group of people who virtually never pray. In their hearts, they don't believe that it works, so they just don't bother.

The Stage 2 group is composed of people who say "now and then" prayers. They are a little embarrassed about prayer, new to the concept, but probably open to learning more. Sometimes they aren't too sure it really works, but they throw a prayer up every now and then.

In the Stage 3 group are people who pray regularly. They talk to God often, they have an ongoing relationship and conversation with Him, and they are intimately connected with Jesus .

In this week's lesson we are going to be looking at two mind-blowing stories from the Bible, one from the Old Testament and one from the New Testament. These stories will help us develop a motivation for prayer. Stage 3 people will be motivated to go deeper, while Stages 1 and 2 people will be motivated to make prayer a regular part of their lives. We all need to dive into prayer and become people who relate to God on a personal level.

The Bible frequently compares us to animals, because too often we act a lot like them. When cattle are being herded from place to place, they have to be urged along with pokes from a sharp stick or an electric cattle prod. Sometimes, we need the same thing. Perhaps these two stories will be a "prayer prod" to get us moving deeper into a life of prayer.

Prayer Prod 1: God is paying attention to those in His family.

Read Luke 18:1-5

This story is one of the most misinterpreted stories in the Bible. Jesus told this parable to His disciples as a "prayer prod." The two characters are a poor widow and an unjust judge. In that day, a woman without a husband or father to take care of her was at the mercy of unscrupulous people. Jesus described the judge as an evil man who didn't care a thing about God or people. When the judge refused the widow justice, she determined to become his worst nightmare. She was going to pester and badger him, never leaving him alone until he gave her what she needed. Finally, the judge became sick of her annoying persistence, and gave her the justice she asked for. He did what was right just to get her off his back. End of story.

So, do you feel motivated to pray now? Is the moral of this story: "It pays to pester"? Many Christians read this story, and assume it is an allegory about us and God. We are like the widow, with no power and no one to turn to. God is like the judge, mean and cruel. Thus, if we bother and pester God long enough we will get what we want, right? That can't be right, can it? Read the next two verses to see what Jesus intended from the story.

Read Luke 18:6-8

Jesus explained Himself at the end of His parable. He told us to listen to the unjust judge's response, and then contrast that judge's character with the character of God. Further, He indicated that we are God's "chosen" (if we know Christ personally and have trusted Him as our Savior). We are adopted into His family as co-heirs with the Lord Jesus, to rule and reign forever in glory.

We are not like the widow, but just the opposite. We have special privilege with the Father, so we are not a bother. We don't have to shout and bang on the door to get His attention. And, God is not like the judge. He loves us. We matter to Him. He wants to give us things, to bless us with His magnificent resources. This theme of God caring for and blessing His chosen children runs throughout the Old Testament. This theme continues into the New Testament, crystallizing with Romans 8:16-17. "The Spirit himself testifies with our spirit that we are God's children. Now if we are children, then we are heirs—heirs of God and co-heirs with Christ, if indeed we share in His sufferings in order that we may also share in His glory."

3. How deeply committed do you think God is to His children? What is the inheritance that God has planned for us?

4. What does it mean to share in Christ's suffering?

This parable of the persistent widow should motivate us to pray for two reasons. First, it reminds us that God is not like the unjust judge. God is interested in our prayers because He is supremely and infinitely interested in us. Second, this story reminds us that God is able, unlimited. We sometimes think that surely He is too busy with greater matters to be bothered with us. If even a corrupt judge will finally answer a persistent plea, how much more our loving heavenly Father will answer His children when they come to Him with requests. He wants us to keep on asking. He doesn't have a limit on the number of meetings we can have with Him each week. He won't tell us we have overrun our quota of prayer requests. Jesus told this parable to demonstrate that we should always pray in faith expecting a loving response from our Father.

5. If faith is defined as trusting God to answer, how would you rate your faith right now?

- ❑ I have faltering faith
- ❑ I have growing faith
- ❑ I have steady faith

Prayer Prod 2: God gives supernatural victory to people who pray.

Read Exodus 17:8-16

Are you ready to be prodded again? The implications of this story might rattle some spiritual cages, but it is clear that God releases His prevailing power into the lives of people who pray. Moses and his people were unmistakably demonstrating their total dependence on God for victory. God punctuated the demonstration by removing His power and blessing each time Moses dropped the connection with Him.

If we pray, symbolically lifting our hands to heaven, and appeal in faith to God for help, it can dramatically turn the tide of the battle we are facing. As we trust God, we begin to see His supernatural power unleashed in our lives.

Conversely, if we don't pray, if we don't ask for God's prevailing power to be released in us, we should not be surprised when the tide of the battle turns against us. At that point, we might feel overwhelmed, defeated, discouraged, and despised. Yet, if we are not calling on God, we will not know how He wants to deal with us, lead us, or work through us. We have cut off communication with the master commander, so we are waging war in hand-to-hand combat when we could have access to the most awesome power in the universe.

When we pray regularly, systematically, fervently, God will work in amazing ways both in and through us. God wants to act in our lives. In Matthew 7:7 Jesus instructs "Ask and it will be given to you, seek and you will find, knock and the door will be opened to you." The Lord wants us to invite His direct involvement in our lives, personal struggles, and spiritual battles.

6. **What are some physical expressions that you use to symbolize your dependence on God when you pray?**

Read Ephesians 6:10-18

7. Are you accustomed to thinking of life in terms of a spiritual battle? Who are we battling against? What are their weapons? What are ours?

8. What part does prayer play in this battle (see verse 18)?

Lift It Up

The story didn't end with Moses standing on the mountain, arms raised to heaven. His arms got tired, but he didn't give up. He didn't try to make it on his own. He called his friends to come and help. Aaron and Hur held up Moses' weary arms. This is exactly what we need to do when we are overwhelmed in prayer or in life. We need to call on our friends to pray with us. We need other believers to stand by us, to motivate, support, and challenge us to pray as we have never prayed before. Isn't it time we began to really pray?

9. Where do you need a couple of friends to hold up your arms? How can this group join in praying with you for this situation?

Take time now to lift each other up as you wage spiritual warfare.

My Prayer Needs:

My Group's Prayer Needs:

"What happens is God's business. Remain faithful no matter what. … our business"

before session six

DEVOTIONALS

Day 1: Matthew 21:21-22

Jesus replied, "I tell you the truth, if you have faith and do not doubt, not only can you do what was done to the fig tree, but also you can say to this mountain, 'Go, throw yourself into the sea,' and it will be done. If you believe, you will receive whatever you ask for in prayer."

Jesus' promise about the prayer of faith being answered seems a little hard to grasp. Why should God answer a prayer about a mountain being thrown into the sea? Surely we can't make God answer us just by "having enough faith." The point is not how much faith you have, but who you have faith in. Why should you waste time asking for something from someone that you don't think is able to do what you ask? If you have faith in the God who can do all things, then whatever you ask for—anything that is in line with His good and perfect will—can and will be done.

Do you have faith that God can and will answer your prayers? What kinds of doubts do you struggle with?

Day 2: John 14:14

You may ask me for anything in my name, and I will do it.

This is a fantastic promise—but it also gives us a hint to explain the confusing problem of why it seems that this promise isn't always fulfilled. Saying the phrase, "In Jesus' name" at the end of every prayer is so strongly ingrained in "Christian culture" that many of us don't even give it a second thought. We believe we are praying "in Jesus' name," but every one of us has asked Him for something that He has not given to us. Why would this be?

Maybe we need to rethink the "in Jesus' name" part of our prayers. Instead of just tacking it on as a "magic formula," we need to think about what it really means. We have free access to God because of Jesus. We are considered clean before God because of Jesus. We have an inheritance in heaven because of Jesus. When we bring our prayer requests before God and ask Him to answer us because of Jesus, we are asking Him to remember Jesus' payment for our sins. We are saying, "Because of Him, I know You, God. He bought me, and I am Yours. I am asking for this because of Jesus." Do you think that the things you are asking for merit being tagged with "because of Jesus"?

When you are asking God for the things you think you need or want, think about whether these are things that will glorify God before you ask "in Jesus' name."

Day 3: 1 John 5:14-15

This is the confidence we have in approaching God: that if we ask anything according to his will, he hears us. And if we know that he hears us—whatever we ask—we know that we have what we asked of him.

Here we find the key to praying with faith. When we are asking for something that is according to God's will, we will surely receive it. God won't ever give us something that is wrong for us to have, or something that will harm us or destroy His work, just because we asked for it and believed we would get it. We are not in danger of spoiling things because of a silly prayer request. God won't be manipulated into doing our will instead of His. Instead, we can be confident and positive that when we pray, He always hears us. As we come to know Him more, we will have much more wisdom about what to pray. We will learn how to ask according to His will. Knowing that He always hears and always answers, we can be secure in the knowledge that He has already prepared the answers for us, and we will receive them at the right time.

We learn to ask according to His will by getting to know Him. We learn to know Him by reading His Word and communicating through prayer. Are you being faithful to read the Bible regularly?

Day 4: Hebrews 11:1

Now faith is being sure of what we hope for and certain of what we do not see.

We wish for many things in life, but we can be sure of what God has promised. Those are the things we can hope for. Our hope is not a wistful wishing for something unsure. We hope in the sense that we are looking forward to something positive that hasn't happened yet, but that we know is coming. It is like hoping for morning after a dark night, or for spring after a long, cold winter. We know it will come. God promised that "as long as the earth endures, seedtime and harvest, cold and heat, summer and winter, day and night will never cease" (Genesis 8:22). We don't see any of what we hope for, but we are certain that it will come ... if God has promised it. It is this kind of faith that God commends and honors.

Why are you sure of what you hope for?

Day 5: James 5:17-18

Elijah was a man just like us. He prayed earnestly that it would not rain, and it did not rain on the land for three and a half years. Again he prayed, and the heavens gave rain, and the earth produced its crops.

Often people hear the stories of the Old Testament heroes, or the New Testament saints, and say, "Well, things were different then. Those people were special." We think that only people of exceptional ability can be used by God. Ordinary people like us are left to do the dull, plodding work. But listen to what James said: "Elijah was a man, just like us." He was an ordinary man, and God used him in an extraordinary way. Elijah was committed to doing whatever God asked him to, even if it was hard. He listened for God's leading, and he prayed the way God told him to. As a result, God was glorified, and Elijah saw God's power at work in amazing ways!

Read 1 Kings 17 to see more ways that God used this "ordinary man."

Day 6: Ephesians 6:18

Pray in the Spirit on all occasions with all kinds of prayers and requests. With this in mind, be alert and always keep on praying for all the saints.

We pray prayers of supplication (asking), thanksgiving, praise, and confession. God wants us to pray all kinds of prayers, to talk to Him about everything that troubles us or brings us joy. We are free to talk to Him at any time, "on all occasions." We pray for ourselves and our needs. But, God also wants us to pray for one another. We are commanded to love one another. When we love one another, we will care about what is happening to each person, and naturally bring one another's problems before God.

Do you pray for other people? Make a list of people to pray for, and take a few minutes each day to go through part of that list.

Day 7: Colossians 1:9

For this reason, since the day we heard about you, we have not stopped praying for you and asking God to fill you with the knowledge of his will through all spiritual wisdom and understanding.

Intercessory prayer is prayer that is on behalf of someone else. Scripture is full of examples of intercessory prayer. Abraham pleaded with God for the righteous of Sodom and Gomorrah. When the Israelites rebelled in the wilderness, Moses pleaded with God over and over for His punishments to be lifted and their lives spared. Jesus prayed for His disciples, and Paul's letters are full of examples of his prayers for the believers. While no one can produce a spiritual life for another person through prayer, God has ordained prayer as a means of helping one another. God could of course carry out all His plans without including us at all, but for some reason He has chosen to give us the joy of knowing and caring about what He is doing for other people. We can participate in a significant way through intercessory prayer.

Paul apparently had not even met the believers in Colosse, and yet he prayed for them. Who are some people that you do not know personally, yet you can pray for?

Day 8: Colossians 1:10-12

And we pray this in order that you may live a life worthy of the Lord and may please him in every way: bearing fruit in every good work, growing in the knowledge of God, being strengthened with all power according to his glorious might so that you may have great endurance and patience, and joyfully giving thanks to the Father, who has qualified you to share in the inheritance of the saints in the kingdom of light.

Sometimes we may pray for someone else that we know and love, asking God to move in a situation that touches us deeply. But many times, intercessory prayers will have nothing to do with us at all. Sometimes people will ask you to pray, and sometimes God will bring a person or situation to your mind and lead you to pray about it. Intercessory prayer is something that will enhance and deepen your relationship with God.

It is usually easy to pray for ourselves. We are well acquainted with our own problems and struggles, and we can think of hundreds of things to ask for. Praying for those we don't know well is much harder. How can we pray according to God's will? How can we pray for the things that they really need most? Look at how Paul prayed for the believers in Colosse. He had never met most of them, but he prayed earnestly for things that he knew would be in the will of God. He couldn't pray for their personal problems, but he could pray for God to give them the tools to deal with these problems. He didn't know what trials they were going through, but he could pray for a relationship with God which would strengthen them in any trial.

Write down a list of the basic things that Paul prayed for these believers. When you don't know how to pray for someone, go back to this list. You can always pray for someone to develop a deeper relationship with Christ.

Day 9: James 5:14-16

Is any one of you sick? He should call the elders of the church to pray over him and anoint him with oil in the name of the Lord. And the prayer offered in faith will make the sick person well; the Lord will raise him up. If he has sinned, he will be forgiven. Therefore confess your sins to each other and pray for each other so that you may be healed. The prayer of a righteous man is powerful and effective.

We aren't used to thinking this way. When one of us is sick, we call in the surgeons, the specialists, the grief counselors, and the psychologists. As an afterthought, we call on a few people to pray. This is not to say that there is anything wrong with using doctors. God has blessed us with modern medicine, and many times He uses these earthly methods rather than miraculous healing. At the same time, why is God our last visit instead of our first?

This kind of situation is one in which intercessory prayer is sometimes used by God in an extraordinary way. But sometimes, He will still answer "No" to our requests for physical healing. If it is your time to die, God won't keep you on this earth any longer than He has decided to. But He still wants us to ask in faith, acknowledging that He is the one in control. One of the ways we can best love and care for one another, is by praying for one another, both for physical and for spiritual healing.

Have you ever seen God answer "Yes" to a prayer of healing? How has this motivated you to keep praying?

Day 10: Acts 12:5

So Peter was kept in prison, but the church was earnestly praying to God for him.

We believe, we are sure of what we hope for, and we pray, but sometimes we are still surprised when God answers. Peter had been thrown in prison for preaching the gospel. Naturally the believers began to pray for him. They doubtless prayed for comfort, and for safety, and for God to arrange for him to be released. Probably, they imagined God influencing Herod to release him, or Peter being acquitted at his trial. They weren't prepared at all for what actually happened.

One evening they were gathered together to pray. As they prayed, God sent an angel into the prison. He kicked Peter to wake him up, the chains fell off, and the angel told Peter to get dressed and follow him out of the prison. Peter obeyed, imagining he was dreaming. He didn't expect this kind of miracle any more than the other believers did. When the cold night air struck his face, and he finally realized that God had answered the prayers of the believers, Peter rushed off to where the believers were praying. When he knocked and asked to be let in, at first no one believed it was actually Peter. They were praying to God for his release, they believed that God was powerful, but He still surprised them when He answered in such a powerful way.

God hardly ever answers in just the way we expect Him to. When you pray for miracles, keep your eyes and ears open. God's best answer probably won't look anything like you imagined.

session six

SMALL-GROUP SESSION

Intercessory Prayer: Praying with Power for Others

Romans 8:33-35; 1 Timothy 2:1-2; Galatians 6:2; Matthew 5:44; John 17:20-26; Ephesians 3:14-21;

As we continue to grow in understanding and to embrace the concept that prayer is about a relationship with God, we learn to pray to God as our Father, not as some detached deity. Prayer becomes more than asking for what we want—it also encompasses praising, repenting, and yielding to Him. God isn't asking us for polished literary genius—even messy prayers go straight to His throne. He is ready to straighten us out, clean us up, and heal our wounds. Though He won't always answer "Yes," we can be sure that He never ignores us. As our relationship and prayers deepen, we begin to pray the hard things, such as asking God to peel off the layers of sin and selfishness in our lives. God wants us to persist, to keep praying and never give up. Even if we don't get the response we're expecting, we trust that He heard, He cares, and He will do the best thing—so we press on in prayer. Pray until you hear from God. He wants us to communicate with Him, and He with us.

The powerful effect of prayer is amplified as we pray for one another. Prayer is about relationship, healing, and life change as we yield to the Lord. Prayer sparks personal growth, but it is also a tool and a resource—a mysteriously powerful agent—for doing good to others. God wants us not only to pray for our own problems, but also to intercede for others.

Start It Up

The word "intercede" means "to beg or plead on behalf of another; to mediate." In other words, an intercessor (one who intercedes) is someone who gets involved in a problem for the sake of someone else. An intercessor tries to help solve a situation that he did not create.

1. **When you hear the word "intercessor," what kind of person comes to mind?**

2. **When you are in a difficult situation, do you find it easy or difficult to ask for help? What sort of person would you ask?**

Talk It Up

Most of us, when we are in a difficult situation, have asked someone else, "would you please pray for me?" But how exactly do you pray "for" someone else? If prayer is for building a personal relationship with God, we cannot have a relationship "for" someone else.

Our Example for Intercession

Through looking at Jesus, the greatest intercessor, we can begin to grasp the concept of intercessory prayer.

Before Jesus' birth, the Jewish people looked forward to the coming of the Messiah—the "anointed one," who would rescue Israel and restore its relationship with God. But the Messiah also came to open the way for all people to relate to God.

When God created the world, Adam and Eve talked with God freely; there was no barrier between them. But God is a Holy God, and He can't be in the presence of sin. So, when the pair in the garden sinned, fellowship was broken. They were no longer free to commune with God. To make matters worse, there was and is no way that sin-scarred humans can make themselves right before God. We don't have the power.

God could have left us dead in our sins like that, but that is not His way. "The LORD looked and was displeased that there was no justice. He saw that there was no one, he was appalled that there was no one to intervene; so his own arm worked salvation for him, and his own righteousness sustained him" (Isaiah 59:15b-16). God knew that we needed someone to intercede for us, someone to set things right between Himself and man.

Only one person could ever be that perfect intercessor. Jesus, the only Son of God, came down to this earth as a human being, and "he poured out his life unto death, and was numbered with the transgressors. For he bore the sin of many, and made intercession for the transgressors" (Isaiah 53:12). Because of Jesus' death, we can come before God with an eternal tag that reads, "Redeemed ... Paid in Full." He interceded for us, paying the price for our sins that we could never pay. Now God looks at us, and sees the perfect blood and sacrifice of His Son instead of our sins and inadequacies.

3. **Knowing that God was willing to make this sacrifice for you, what does this tell you about Him?**

Read Romans 8:33-35

Jesus not only gave His life for us on the cross, but He continues to give up His life for us as He intercedes for us—pleads on our behalf—in God's courtroom.

It is easy to see how Jesus could pray for us. He is our intercessor, the one who makes it possible for us to come before God. He is God's perfect Son.. For Jesus, the Intercessor, praying for others makes sense. But what about us?

Just like Jesus, when we intercede in prayer, we lay aside our own agendas so that we can help in a situation or problem that we did not create. Because Jesus' sacrifice paved the way for us, we can go boldly before the throne of God as His children. We cannot take the place of the other person before God, but we can be a representative—an advocate. Our motivation to intercede for someone else is love. Because we have experienced Christ's never-ending love, we overflow with love for other people.

4. **Can you describe a time when someone else has prayed on your behalf, and how that made you feel?**

Our Motivation for Intercession

Read 1 Timothy 2:1-2 and Galatians 6:2

We are familiar with the prayers, requests, and thanksgiving mentioned in these verses to Timothy, but what does it mean to make intercession for others? How can we carry each other's "burdens"? A vital way to do that is through intercessory prayer: praying for the needs of others. What better way to express love for one another than interceding in prayer with the almighty God of the universe? A key component of Jesus' prayer for all believers is that we would be unified in love (John 17:23). God wants us to talk to Him, not only about our own needs but about the needs of those we love. Love can only be demonstrated within the context of community, love must be the hallmark of our faith.

Read Matthew 5:44

We are commanded to take our prayers one step further beyond praying for those we love. God also commands us to pray for our enemies. That is a true test of love: when you are willing to pray for someone who has hurt you—someone you may not even like. Most of the time, we pray intercessory prayers because we have been asked to. People approach us, explain their needs or problems, and ask us to join in praying with or for them. This is good, and a part of the way God intends for His people to love and care for one another. At other times, however, intercessory prayer may have a different beginning. You may find yourself praying earnestly for someone you don't even know, or for a situation you really know nothing about. Have you ever awakened suddenly in the middle of the night, thinking about a certain person or situation? This may be God nudging you to pray for that person. You might find that God prods you to prayer by making a situation or person "alive" to you. Don't just pass over these opportunities—God has allowed you to feel the pain or the burden of the problem just so that you can pray at that time.

We may be tempted to sidestep praying for others because we doubt the power of prayer or because we do not fully understand exactly what happens in intercessory prayer, but the Bible assures us that "The prayer of a righteous man is powerful and effective" (James 5:16).

5. **How has God nudged you to pray for someone?**

Our Pattern for Intercession

There are definitely times when we are asked to pray for someone else, or when God nudges us to pray, but we don't really know what to say. Look at and utilize Paul's prayer for the believers in Ephesus as a model when you don't know how else to pray.

In Ephesians 3:16-17a, Paul writes "I pray that out of his glorious riches he may strengthen you with power through his Spirit in your inner being, so that Christ may dwell in your hearts through faith." Paul didn't just pray for strength, he prayed for supernatural strength from the Holy Spirit. Even though we may not know the specifics of the situation we're praying for, we can be sure that we all need God's strength in our lives.

Paul goes on to say in verses 17-19, "And I pray that you, being rooted and established in love, may have power, together with all the saints, to grasp how wide and long and high and deep is the love of Christ, and to know this love that surpasses knowledge—that you may be filled to the measure of all the fullness of God."

What's the bottom line? Paul was praying that they would not only know about God's love, but also experience His love personally.

Lift It Up

Read Ephesians 3:20-21

How cool is it to know that we pray to the One who cannot only meet, but exceed our expectations? What an incredible privilege prayer is, allowing us to have a direct line to the Creator of all things!

6. How will you need to change to make prayer a priority?

7. Have you kept up your prayer journal? If so, share with the group some of your answers to prayer.

Take time to intercede for one another in specific areas of need.

My Prayer Needs:

My Group's Prayer Needs:

June Beulah - Bell & Shalaluna -
Joyce - 0
Charlie -
Hugh - Prayer list
[illegible] - Nancy M.
Bea - 0
Sheryl - Roy & Marilyn - Tom Cosgroove -
[illegible] - George neighbor - Vivian

Det. 200

Leader's Guide

Whether you are a brand new small-group leader or a long-time veteran this leader's guide is designed to help you make the most of your small-group time. It will help you facilitate a healthy discussion among the members of your group as well as provide you with insight and answers to the questions in each session. Remember to check here not only for answers to questions you are not sure about, but also for ideas on how to involve everyone, how to bring creativity to the discussion, and how to delegate leadership to others.

Throughout this study there are a few places where you will encounter large sections of Scripture to be read. As the leader, you should encourage the members of your group to come to your meeting time prepared, having read the chapter, checked the Scripture references, and answered the questions. That way you can summarize these large blocks rather than risk losing people's attention while someone reads aloud. But, be careful not to assume that everyone knows these Bible stories, and make sure your summaries give the important points. Doing this will help you maintain a smooth flow in the discussion as you stay on task and on time in your small group.

Leading a small group can be a challenging experience, but it also brings many rewards, so invest some time in preparing yourself to lead. You will be delighted with the results!

Session One
Prayer Conditioning

1. **Were you taught to pray as a child? Did you learn set prayers to recite, or did you learn to pray spontaneously?**

   A: There will be a variety of answers to this question.

   Tip: For fun, if anyone says they learned set prayers to recite, see if they can still remember and recite them.

2. **How would you rate your "prayer proficiency" now? Do you think that your early training was a help or a hindrance?**

   A: People will have different responses due to their different experiences. Some follow-up questions to enhance the discussion could include:
   - Why do you rate your prayer proficiency as poor/good?
   - What could make it better?

3. **What are some characteristics of good earthly fathers that you have known? In what ways do these men reflect God, the Father?**

   A: Again, everyone will have different answers about what they have experienced. A great way to help the members of your group apply this discussion to their lives is to write down the list of qualities people bring up and how they reflect God. Type up the list and e-mail or distribute it to the group for future reference as you all seek to be a clearer reflection of your heavenly Father.

4. **Do you see the Lord's Prayer in Matthew 6 as something that we should recite verbatim, or as a model prayer from which we should build our prayers? Why?**

   A: This question can provide your group with some great discussion. There is not an absolute right or wrong answer. It is certainly okay to repeat The Lord's Prayer verbatim, but it should not be our exclusive communication with God. Jesus gave this model for the disciples and for us to follow:

   - Verse 9 – praise God
   - Verse 10 – pray for God's work and His perfect plan in this world and the next
   - Verse 11 – recognize God as the Provider
   - Verse 12 – appeal to God for forgiveness of sin
   - Verse 13 – seek protection from temptation and the evil one, Satan

5. **What do you think a life with real "prayer priority" would look like?**

   A: People who prioritize prayer are those who have a regular time alone with God. They may pray in their car, as they read the Bible, sit quietly and 'listen' for God, or perhaps all of the above. When you practice this priority regularly it becomes apparent in your life. You will notice a greater sense of peace and contentment, less stress and anger, and an overall better outlook on life.

6. **What might be some other advantages of a personal "prayer closet"? What places have you found that make good "closets"?**

   A: Personal prayer closets provide us with a place to go and shut out the distractions of the world and get real with God.

7. **How can we avoid "babbling" when we pray? What might this look like?**

   A: One way to avoid babbling in prayer is to enter into it with a plan. A good pattern we can use is the P-R-A-Y acronym outlined in the session. Another option is to write out your prayers. Since writing takes longer than speaking, we tend to be more concise when we write.

8. **Since God knows what we need before we ask for it, why do we need to ask? How does this knowledge affect how we pray?**

   A: Asking God to meet our needs serves at least two purposes. First, it establishes communication between God and us. That line of communication is essential to our spiritual health and growth. Second, it is a way for us to acknowledge our full dependence on God as our Provider. Knowing these things should help us be more confident and more concise in our prayers since we know that God already knows our needs and has promised to meet them if they are in line with His will.

9. **Regular prayer is not easy even for Christians. What barriers keep you from praying the way you need to for yourself and for others?**

   A: Of course, each person's response will vary, but you might suggest things such as time, busyness, not knowing how to pray, worry about approaching God, in our inadequacies, and lack of faith right now.

10. **Praying together for each other's needs is an important part of doing life together. In what way can this group pray for you right now and throughout the week?**

    Tip: Encourage the group to be purposeful about praying for one another in the time between your gatherings. To help facilitate this, you may want to have people write their requests on an index card as they share them. Then, they can pass them to the person on their right to be prayed for throughout the week. Feel free to be creative! You can also encourage people to write prayer requests in the space provided in their books.

Session Two
Vertical Reality

1. **Describe a friendship you have in which you feel comfortable going beyond surface level. How many people are in this close circle of friends?**

Tip: As people describe these relationships listen for commonalities. Before moving on, point out the common threads you notice.

2. **For you, what is the dividing line between "surface-level" and "deep" conversation? How often do you dive in?**

Tip: The different answers to this question will help you understand the people in your group better. Depth, for many, is becoming intellectual. For others it is sharing emotionally. Still others find depth in relationships where they can sit comfortably in silence. Whatever the answer, you can learn a lot about how to relate to a person if you understand how they view depth.

3. **Do you consider yourself an introspective person? What are the dangers of not examining yourself? What are the dangers of too much self-examination?**

A: The dangers of living a life with no self-examination are ignorance and stagnant growth. On the other hand, too much self-examination can cause "paralysis of analysis," which leaves people bogged down in trying to figure out the "whys" and "how tos" rather than just making a change and moving on.

4. **How can healthy self-examination make your prayers different?**

A: A healthy look at your life will open your eyes to your strengths and weaknesses. It will let you see where you have room to grow. All of that adds up to clearer, more powerful, more specific prayers.

5. **Does praying a transparent prayer feel safe to you? Why or why not?**

Tip: Be prepared for both "yes" and "no" answers by having a follow-up question in mind for each. Good follow-up questions help keep the discussion alive and on topic. You might ask, "What has helped you the most as you have learned to open up with God?" Or, for the negative answer, "Is there any way that our group can support you as you begin to open up more to God?"

6. **How can we be transparent and still keep from charging God with wrongdoing?**

A: It all depends on your attitude and the condition of your heart. Approach God honestly, yet with humility and a desire to learn from Him. If you attack Him as though you are some superior intelligence, arrogantly demanding His response, how do you suppose He might respond?

7. **What other scriptural promises, or examples of God's work in your past, can you think of that would give you confidence in praying transparently?**

   A: Some examples from Scripture include: 1 John 1:9, Psalm 13:5, and Isaiah 54:10.

8. **Should anyone other than God hear your transparent prayers? Why or why not?**

   A: It is definitely important to be real and transparent with other people. This kind of vulnerability can build trust and strengthen relationships. However, we need to be careful of our motives. Don't pray transparently to impress others with your spirituality (see Matthew 6:5) or to manipulate or hurt them.

9. **What techniques can you think of that might help with listening? What can you do to keep your mind from wandering?**

   A: A few ways to help learn the discipline of listening are:
   (1) Go somewhere with no distractions.
   (2) Speak briefly to God, and then ask Him for a few moments of mental peace and quiet to listen for Him.
   (3) Practice meditation (no, not the lotus position, mantra-moaning meditation!). Biblical meditation is reading a verse and really "chewing on" it—repeating it over and over to yourself, asking God to speak to you through it.

10. **In your prayer life, a few small tweaks can help you dive so much deeper. What are some tweaks you have discovered that you need to make?**

    A: Reviewing the key points from this session consider these tweaks:
    (1) Commit to regular reflection and self-examination.
    (2) Risk pouring out your hurt, pain, and struggles to God.
    (3) Recall God's character and active involvement in your life.
    (4) Resolve to trust God no matter how tough life gets.
    (5) Take more time to really listen to God.

Session Three
A Bad Prayer Day

1. **What is one thing you wanted desperately when you were a child? Who did you ask for it? Did you get it?**

   Tip: This question should generate some fun, lighthearted conversation and get everyone involved.

2. **Looking back on it now, would you say it was good, bad, or neutral that you did (or didn't) get what you wanted?**

   Tip: This is a great time to use some of those follow-up questions like "Why?" or "What do you think might have happened if you had/had not received that item?" Be creative and have fun ... the idea is just to get people talking.

3. **Since God sometimes does say "No," what does the promise in Luke 11:9-10 mean when it says, "Ask and it will be given you"?**

   A: When reading Scripture verses it is important to remember that we have to look at them in the context of all of Scripture. In this case, the promise seems to be that if we ask God, He will give us whatever we want. Looking at this promise in the overall context of Scripture, though, shows us that He will only give us what is in His perfect will for us (see 1 John 5:14).

4. **How should we approach planning for the future? Should we make plans at all? Check out James 4:13-15 for some ideas.**

   A: Planning for our future is something we should all do. The key is to approach those plans with the right attitude, understanding that God's plans are superior to any we will ever make. We cannot take for granted that the plans we lay out will be in line with the plans our Father has, so we must be flexible and follow His lead, even when it means altering or even abandoning our plans.

5. **How have you experienced the fact that God is loving, just, and will do the best thing?**

   Tip: Remember that people will usually only be as open and personal as the leader of the group. This is a time when you can show some vulnerability and encourage the group members to "go deeper" by your example.

6. **What are some inappropriate prayers we pray?**

   A: Nearly everyone has prayed one of these prayers before. Things like, "God, if you will just let me win the lottery ..." or "Please God, make him love me ..." and a personal favorite for many, "Alright God, if you'll just get me out of trouble this time, I promise I'll never do this again!" One way to help us ensure we are praying appropriately is to ask God to align our will with His, even if it means giving up on something we really want.

7. **In your everyday life, what is one thing you hate to wait on? How do you react?**

   Tip: This is a question that everyone can get involved in, even if they don't know a thing about the Bible. Be real, have fun, and encourage one another to get a grip when it comes to waiting ... especially on God!

8. **How do you react when you have to wait on God?**

   Tip: This question is included as a follow-up to the previous question. It will help us realize how silly it is for the created thing (us) to get frustrated and shake our puny fists at the Creator.

9. **Why does God require us to resolve our conflicts with others in order to keep our prayer connection with Him?**

   A: Our prayer connection with God is affected by our relationships with others because God created us to first love Him, but also to love others (see Matthew 22:37-39). We cannot be in harmony with God if we have disharmony with His other children.

10. **What is a prayer that you are waiting to have answered? How has this study helped you understand why you don't have an answer yet?**

   Tip: The "rubber meets the road" here. Encourage personal application through this question. Reminders: God has the master plan and a purpose in everything, keeps us from trouble when we pray for "bad" things or with wrong motives, sets His clock differently, and plugs His ears when we have sin or relational issues.

Session Four
For Mature Audiences Only

1. **How old were you when you learned to swim? Do you like deep water, or would you rather stay in the wading pool?**

   Tip: Have fun with this question, but you may use it to point out how our past experiences can affect us today.

2. **How do you feel about other kinds of risks and dangers? Are you more likely to take physical risks or emotional/relational risks?**

   Tip: Again, keep this lighthearted. Do not probe too deeply at this point in the session. The study will naturally take your group into deeper issues during your time together.

3. **Once you have prayed, "examine me," what should you do with what God shows you? What can happen if God shows you something that is wrong in your life and you continue to ignore it?**

   A: When God reveals a character flaw in you, the first thing you need to do is confess it. Own up to God that you are out of line. Then, repent—turn away from whatever it is. If you ignore what God shows you and continue in your sin, every part of your life will be negatively affected, even areas that don't seem related. Refusing to allow God to control one area of your life is refusing to allow Him to control your life as a whole. Our lives can't be compartmentalized.

4. **When you pray, "break me," what is your responsibility in the process? Are you supposed to sit back and wait for God to act, or is there something you should do? If so, what?**

   A: Look at Zaccheus as an example. When Jesus showed him his sin, Zaccheus was broken. He went out and tried to make right what he had been done. We all have a responsibility to respond to God when He shows us our sins and breaks their stranglehold on us.

5. **How can we recognize a test from God when we see it? What is the difference between testing and the normal problems we face in everyday life?**

   A: Realize that God may not show us that we are being tested. In that case, we just need to be obedient to God and His reshaping of our lives in the situation. Ask yourself a few strategic questions to see if there is something God wants to teach or develop in you:
   - Am I being unfaithful to God in any area of my life?
   - Is there anything I should be doing that I am not?
   - Is there anything I am doing and should not be?

   If you can answer yes to any of these questions, you may be in the midst of a test.

6. **In what ways does God guide? Since He usually doesn't speak audibly, or send us step-by-step instruction manuals in the mail, how can we learn to recognize His guidance?**

   A: God uses many methods to lead and guide us. He speaks to us through other believers, through those in authority over us, through the Bible, and through the Holy Spirit. The challenge is that too often we are not listening for God in the way He is choosing to communicate with us. We tend to want "signs" or dramatic directions, but God often speaks to us in "whispers" and subtle suggestions.

7. **What is a personal experience you have had (good or bad) that God could or did use to impact others?**

   Tip: This is a very strong question and may bring some very emotional responses. If others seem hesitant to answer, this is one of the times you may want to speak first. Leave plenty of time for people who want to share an experience to be able to. Encourage everyone to use their unique experiences to communicate God's grace to others.

8. **Consider the people in your group. What are some qualities in them that you could see God using for His purposes?**

   Tip: Set the tone for answering this question by establishing that it is not a time for empty flattery. Instead, use this opportunity to recognize each person's unique gifts, life experiences, and personality. Share with them how they have affected you or how you can see them influencing others for God's purposes.

9. **Even the most "open-minded" people will find out sooner or later that God's way of thinking is different from anything they have ever experienced. When has God stretched your thinking, and taught you something that "went against the grain" of your thought patterns?**

   Tip: Read Isaiah 55:8-9. God explains that we will not understand everything as He does, but that we should trust that His way is better than ours. This trust, or faith, is the key to being stretched and grown.

10. **Together, ask God for courage to pray these deep-water prayers. Is there some area of your life, or a difficult situation that needs special help? Share these needs with the group, and pray together for God's help and guidance.**

    Tip: Some people in your group may risk being open and share very emotional or disturbing issues. Do not push for this, but if it occurs, be sure to demonstrate love and compassion. You might invite them to stick around after your meeting to talk and pray further. Refer any difficult issues to your pastor or a qualified Christian counselor.

Session Five
Blown Away

1. **Who do you feel listens and responds to you the best? What makes you choose this person?**

Tip: Good follow-up questions will make this simple "warm-up" question a great topic of conversation. Try things like, "How does that person listen differently than someone else?" or "What makes your connection with this person work?" Be creative and come up with some simple follow-ups that will get a conversation going.

2. When you feel you have something important to communicate, would you rather talk or write? Why?

Tip: You can have fun as a group taking a time-out here to write a few lines to someone important. It may be a prayer to God, a thank-you to a friend, or a love note to your spouse. When everyone finishes they should tell the group whom they wrote to and why. They do not need to share what they wrote.

3. How deeply committed do you think God is to His children? What is the inheritance that God has planned for us?

A: The Bible says that the angels look at the relationship that God has with us, His children, and they just marvel at it. Christians can look forward to inheriting eternal life in heaven, and all that comes with it.

4. What does it mean to share in Christ's suffering?

A: Sharing in Christ's suffering refers to the persecution of Christians in different parts of the world throughout history and today. Though we may not live in a society that oppresses or persecutes Christ-followers, we still pay a price by giving up our own rights to serve others. That price is nothing compared to the price God paid for us with His only Son, though. Our suffering can draw us closer to Christ because we know He understands what we are experiencing.

5. If faith is defined as trusting God to answer, how would you rate your faith right now?

- **I have faltering faith**
- **I have growing faith**
- **I have steady faith**

Tip: Ask the members to identify whatever level of faith they place themselves in. Then, ask for ideas about how to increase our faith.

6. **What are some physical expressions that you use to symbolize your dependence on God when you pray?**

   A: Different people will have different ways, such as raising their hands toward heaven, kneeling, clasping their hands together and bowing their heads, etc. To put this into practice, as people are physically able, have them kneel together and pray at the end of your meeting.

7. **Are you accustomed to thinking of life in terms of a spiritual battle? Who are we battling against? What are their weapons? What are ours?**

   A: Spiritual battle rages all around us every day and, even though we don't always know it, we are participants. The enemy is Satan and his demonic army. They attack us with flaming arrows in the form of lies, doubt, fear, and temptation. The armor of God is described in Ephesians 6:14-17. The idea of an unseen battle in the spiritual realm is hard for some people to swallow, but the Bible is clear on this. The first step in fighting the battle is recognizing that it exists.

8. **What part does prayer play in this battle (see verse 18)?**

   A: Prayer is our connection to God, the Commander in Chief. He provides us with protection, strategy, and strength for the fight. Leaving out prayer would be like entering a war zone and forgetting to communicate with your commanding officer.

9. **Where do you need a couple of friends to hold up your arms? How can this group join in praying with you for this situation?**

   Tip: As people express specific needs, gather around them as a group and lay your hands on them as you pray. The Bible encourages this physical contact, plus it will encourage the people you are praying for.

Session Six
Intercessory Prayer

1. **When you hear the work "intercessor," what kind of person comes to mind?**

   Tip: Remind the group that God calls us all to be intercessors. For some, this may be a special focus of caring for and serving others, but that does not mean that the rest of us are off the hook.

2. **When you are in a difficult situation, do you find it easy or difficult to ask for help? What sort of person would you ask?**

   Tip: Try to get people to explain their answers about asking for help. If it is easy, how do they go about it? If it is hard, why? When talking about the kind of person people would ask for help, make a list of qualities as people give answers. Challenge everyone to become a person others will trust, a person with the qualities listed..

3. **Knowing that God was willing to make this sacrifice for you, what does this tell you about Him?**

   A: We clearly see that He is faithful, compassionate, and forgiving. He is love.

4. **Can you describe a time when someone else has prayed on your behalf, and how that made you feel?**

   Tip: Good follow-ups are, "Did you know they were doing it at the time?" and "How did it make you feel to know someone was praying/had prayed for you? Why did you feel that way?"

5. **How has God nudged you to pray for someone?**

   Tip: There should be as many different answers to this question as there are people in your group. Point out how God uses different ways to get our attention, emphasizing the need to listen carefully and to respond when God nudges us.

6. **How will you need to change to make prayer a priority?**

   Tip: As group members share their answers, ask them how they will make sure that this change takes place in their lives. Also, ask them to share one way their prayer life has been positively affected through this study.

7. **Have you kept up your prayer journal? If so, share with the group some of your answers to prayer.**

   Tip: Review again the benefits prayer journal, such as the ability to keep track of other's needs so that you remember to pray; having a tool to help you become more regular and disciplined in prayer; plus the blessing of recording and looking back on the wonderful answers to prayer that God provides you.

Notes

Sheryl & Bea
Jim —
Miriam — eye surg. today
~~Dan~~ Skube
Sis — children

Linda — brother Elgin

Gail — herself

Nan — nancy & husband
3 WKS. Red cross
Heather grandmother

Joyce — family & friends
travel holiday

Elsa — Hugh's B.P.

Hugh — all of the above —
Disaster people —

10 A.M. Brunch 12/14 Sheryl's
Martin Pot Luck Share
Breakfast casserole devotional
not lesson

us Orange juice c champagne

Hallmark store
11 — + 3 A Jim
nancy — aunt

Twins ok granddaug
Prayer 12/ Van funeral
Sheryl. & Bea — family church people Gail — no
Nan — nancy & hus. Elsa — Dan Sk. (Joy Ling) Blanche
June — me — Jim Rex
Nancy — Charlie mike — George
Bea — Teacher friend Joan cay man —